Neural Network Programming with TensorFlow

Unleash the power of TensorFlow to train efficient neural networks

Manpreet Singh Ghotra

Rajdeep Dua

BIRMINGHAM - MUMBAI

Neural Network Programming with TensorFlow

First published: November 2017

Production reference: 1081117

Published by Packt Publishing Ltd.
Livery Place
35 Livery Street
Birmingham
B3 2PB, UK.

ISBN 978-1-78839-039-2

www.packtpub.com

Credits

Authors
Manpreet Singh Ghotra
Rajdeep Dua

Reviewer
Giancarlo Zaccone

Commissioning Editor
Amey Varangaonkar

Acquisition Editor
Varsha Shetty

Content Development Editor
Tejas Limkar

Technical Editor
Sagar Sawant

Copy Editor
Tasneem Fatehi

Project Coordinator
Manthan Patel

Proofreader
Safis Editing

Indexer
Rekha Nair

Graphics
Tania Dutta

Production Coordinator
Aparna Bhagat

About the Authors

Manpreet Singh Ghotra has more than 15 years of experience in software development for both enterprise and big data software. He is currently working on developing a machine learning platform/API's using open source libraries and frameworks like TensorFlow, Keras, Apache Spark and PredictionIO at Salesforce. He has worked on various machine learning systems like sentiment analysis, spam detection, image moderation and anomaly detection. He was part of the machine learning group at one of the largest online retailers in the world, working on transit time calculations using R and Apache Mahout. With a master's and a postgraduate degree in machine learning, he has contributed to and worked for the machine learning community.

His GitHub profile is `https://github.com/badlogicmanpreet` and you can find him on LinkedIn at `https://in.linkedin.com/in/msghotra`.

This book is dedicated to my parents, Amrik Singh and Nirmal Kaur. I would like to thank my family for bearing with me while I spent time writing this book.

Rajdeep Dua has over 18 years of experience in the cloud, big data, and machine learning space. He has worked in the advocacy team for Google's big data tools, BigQuery. He has worked on the Greenplum big data platform at VMware in the developer evangelist team. He also worked closely with a team on porting Spark to run on VMware's public and private cloud as a feature set. He has taught Spark and big data at some of the most prestigious tech schools in India--IIIT Hyderabad, ISB, IIIT Delhi, and College of Engineering, Pune.

Currently, he leads the developer relations team at Salesforce India. He has published numerous blogs and hands-on labs for Einstein, a machine learning library from Salesforce and Apache Prediction IO.

He has published several big data and Spark tutorials at cluddatalab. He has also presented BigQuery and Google App Engine at the W3C conference in Hyderabad. He has led the developer relations teams at Google, VMware, and Microsoft, and he has spoken at hundreds of other conferences on the cloud.

His contributions to the open source community are for Docker, Kubernetes, Android, OpenStack, Prediction IO, and cloudfoundry projects.

> *This book is dedicated to my parents. I would like to thank my wife, Manjula, and sons, Navtej and Kairav, for bearing with me while I spent time writing this book.*

About the Reviewer

Giancarlo Zaccone has more than ten years of experience of managing both scientific and industrial research projects. He has worked as a researcher at the C.N.R, the National Research Council, where he was involved in projects related to parallel numerical computing and scientific visualization.

Currently, he is a senior software engineer at a consulting company, developing and testing software systems for space and defense applications.

Giancarlo holds a master's degree in physics from the Federico II of Naples and a second-level postgraduate master's degree in scientific computing from La Sapienza of Rome.

He is the author of the following Packt books: *Python Parallel Programming Cookbook, Getting Started with TensorFlow,* and *Deep Learning with TensorFlow.*

You can contact him at `https://it.linkedin.com/in/giancarlozaccone.`

www.PacktPub.com

For support files and downloads related to your book, please visit www.PacktPub.com. Did you know that Packt offers eBook versions of every book published, with PDF and ePub files available? You can upgrade to the eBook version at www.PacktPub.com and as a print book customer, you are entitled to a discount on the eBook copy. Get in touch with us at service@packtpub.com for more details. At www.PacktPub.com, you can also read a collection of free technical articles, sign up for a range of free newsletters and receive exclusive discounts and offers on Packt books and eBooks.

https://www.packtpub.com/mapt

Get the most in-demand software skills with Mapt. Mapt gives you full access to all Packt books and video courses, as well as industry-leading tools to help you plan your personal development and advance your career.

Why subscribe?

- Fully searchable across every book published by Packt
- Copy and paste, print, and bookmark content
- On demand and accessible via a web browser

Customer Feedback

Thanks for purchasing this Packt book. At Packt, quality is at the heart of our editorial process. To help us improve, please leave us an honest review on this book's Amazon page at https://www.amazon.in/dp/1788390393. If you'd like to join our team of regular reviewers, you can email us at customerreviews@packtpub.com. We award our regular reviewers with free eBooks and videos in exchange for their valuable feedback. Help us be relentless in improving our products!

Table of Contents

Preface

If you're aware of the buzz surrounding terms such as machine learning, artificial intelligence, or deep learning, you might know what neural networks are. Ever wondered how they help solve complex computational problems efficiently, or how to train efficient neural networks? This book will teach you both of these things, and more.

You will start by getting a quick overview of the popular TensorFlow library and see how it is used to train different neural networks. You will get a thorough understanding of the fundamentals and basic math for neural networks and why TensorFlow is a popular choice. Then, you will proceed to implement a simple feedforward neural network. Next, you will master optimization techniques and algorithms for neural networks using TensorFlow. Further, you will learn how to implement some more complex types of neural networks such as **convolutional neural networks** (**CNNs**), **recurrent neural networks** (**RNNs**), and **Deep Belief Networks** 0;(**DBNs**). In the course of the book, you will be working on real-world datasets to get a hands-on understanding of neural network programming. You will also get to train generative models and will learn the applications of autoencoders.

By the end of this book, you will have a fair understanding of how to leverage the power of TensorFlow to train neural networks of varying complexities, without any hassle.

What this book covers

Chapter 1, *Maths for Neural Networks*, covers the basics of algebra, probability, and optimization techniques for neural networks.

Chapter 2, *Deep Feedforward Networks*, explains the basics of perceptrons, neurons, and feedforward neural networks. You will also learn about various learning techniques and mainly the core learning algorithm called backpropagation.

Chapter 3, *Optimization for Neural Networks*, covers optimization techniques that are fundamental to neural network learning.

Chapter 4, *Convolutional Neural Networks*, discusses the CNN algorithm in detail. CNNs and their application to different data types will also be covered.

Chapter 5, *Recurrent Neural Networks*, covers the RNN algorithm in detail. RNNs and their application to different data types are covered as well.

Chapter 6, *Generative Models*, explains the basics of generative models and the different approaches to generative models.

Chapter 7, *Deep Belief Networking*, covers the basics of deep belief networks, how they differ from the traditional neural networks, and their implementation.

Chapter 8, *Autoencoders*, provides an introduction to autoencoders, which have recently come to the forefront of generative modeling.

Chapter 9, *Deep Learning Research and Summary*, discusses the current and future research details on deep learning. It also points the readers to papers for reference reading.

Appendix, *Getting Started with TensorFlow*, discusses environment setup of TensorFlow, comparison of TensorFlow with NumPy, and the concept if Auto differentiation

What you need for this book

This book will guide you through the installation of all the tools that you need to follow the examples:

- Python 3.4 or above
- TensorFlow r.14 or above

Who this book is for

This book is meant for developers with a statistical background who want to work with neural networks. Though we will be using TensorFlow as the underlying library for neural networks, this book can be used as a generic resource to bridge the gap between the math and the implementation of deep learning. If you have some understanding of Tensorflow and Python and want to learn what happens at a level lower than the plain API syntax, this book is for you.

Conventions

In this book, you will find a number of text styles that distinguish between different kinds of information. Here are some examples of these styles and an explanation of their meaning. Code words in text, database table names, folder names, filenames, file extensions, pathnames, dummy URLs, user input, and Twitter handles are shown as follows: "The next lines of code read the link and assign it to the `BeautifulSoup` function." A block of code is set as follows:

```
#import packages into the project
from bs4 import BeautifulSoup
from urllib.request import urlopen
import pandas as pd
```

When we wish to draw your attention to a particular part of a code block, the relevant lines or items are set in bold:

```
 [default] exten
=> s,1,Dial(Zap/1|30) exten
=> s,2,Voicemail(u100) exten
=> s,102,Voicemail(b100) exten
=> i,1,Voicemail(s0)
```

Any command-line input or output is written as follows:

```
C:\Python34\Scripts> pip install –upgrade pip
C:\Python34\Scripts> pip install pandas
```

New terms and **important words** are shown in bold. Words that you see on the screen, for example, in menus or dialog boxes, appear in the text like this: "In order to download new modules, we will go to **Files | Settings | Project Name | Project Interpreter**."

Warnings or important notes appear like this.

Tips and tricks appear like this.

Reader feedback

Feedback from our readers is always welcome. Let us know what you think about this book-what you liked or disliked. Reader feedback is important for us as it helps us develop titles that you will really get the most out of. To send us general feedback, simply email feedback@packtpub.com, and mention the book's title in the subject of your message. If there is a topic that you have expertise in and you are interested in either writing or contributing to a book, see our author guide at www.packtpub.com/authors.

Customer support

Now that you are the proud owner of a Packt book, we have a number of things to help you to get the most from your purchase.

Downloading the example code

You can download the example code files for this book from your account at http://www.packtpub.com. If you purchased this book elsewhere, you can visit http://www.packtpub.com/support and register to have the files emailed directly to you. You can download the code files by following these steps:

1. Log in or register to our website using your email address and password.
2. Hover the mouse pointer on the **SUPPORT** tab at the top.
3. Click on **Code Downloads & Errata**.
4. Enter the name of the book in the **Search** box.
5. Select the book for which you're looking to download the code files.
6. Choose from the drop-down menu where you purchased this book from.
7. Click on **Code Download**.

Once the file is downloaded, please make sure that you unzip or extract the folder using the latest version of:

- WinRAR / 7-Zip for Windows
- Zipeg / iZip / UnRarX for Mac
- 7-Zip / PeaZip for Linux

The code bundle for the book is also hosted on GitHub at `https://github.com/PacktPublishing/Neural-Network-Programming-with-TensorFlow`. We also have other code bundles from our rich catalog of books and videos available at `https://github.com/PacktPublishing/`. Check them out!

Downloading the color images of this book

We also provide you with a PDF file that has color images of the screenshots/diagrams used in this book. The color images will help you better understand the changes in the output. You can download this file from `https://www.packtpub.com/sites/default/files/downloads/NeuralNetworkProgramming withTensorFlow_ColorImages.pdf`.

Errata

Although we have taken every care to ensure the accuracy of our content, mistakes do happen. If you find a mistake in one of our books-maybe a mistake in the text or the code-we would be grateful if you could report this to us. By doing so, you can save other readers from frustration and help us improve subsequent versions of this book. If you find any errata, please report them by visiting `http://www.packtpub.com/submit-errata`, selecting your book, clicking on the **Errata Submission Form** link, and entering the details of your errata. Once your errata are verified, your submission will be accepted and the errata will be uploaded to our website or added to any list of existing errata under the Errata section of that title. To view the previously submitted errata, go to `https://www.packtpub.com/books/content/support` and enter the name of the book in the search field. The required information will appear under the **Errata** section.

Piracy

Piracy of copyrighted material on the internet is an ongoing problem across all media. At Packt, we take the protection of our copyright and licenses very seriously. If you come across any illegal copies of our works in any form on the internet, please provide us with the location address or website name immediately so that we can pursue a remedy. Please contact us at `copyright@packtpub.com` with a link to the suspected pirated material. We appreciate your help in protecting our authors and our ability to bring you valuable content.

Questions

If you have a problem with any aspect of this book, you can contact us at questions@packtpub.com, and we will do our best to address the problem.

1
Maths for Neural Networks

Neural network users need to have a fair understanding of neural network concepts, algorithms, and the underlying mathematics. Good mathematical intuition and understanding of many techniques is necessary for a solid grasp of the inner functioning of the algorithms and for getting good results. The amount of maths required and the level of maths needed to understand these techniques is multidimensional and also depends on interest. In this chapter, you will learn neural networks by understanding the maths used to solve complex computational problems. This chapter covers the basics of linear algebra, calculus, and optimization for neural networks.

The main purpose of this chapter is to set up the fundamentals of mathematics for the upcoming chapters.

Following topics will be covered in the chapter:

- Understanding linear algebra
- Understanding Calculus
- Optimization

Understanding linear algebra

Linear algebra is a key branch of mathematics. An understanding of linear algebra is crucial for **deep learning**, that is, neural networks. Throughout this chapter, we will go through the key and fundamental linear algebra prerequisites. Linear Algebra deals with linear systems of equations. Instead of working with scalars, we start working with matrices and vectors. Using linear algebra, we can describe complicated operations in deep learning.

Environment setup

Before we jump into the field of mathematics and its properties, it's essential for us to set up the development environment as it will provide us settings to execute the concepts we learn, meaning installing the compiler, dependencies, and **IDE** (**Integrated Development Environment**) to run our code base.

Setting up the Python environment in Pycharm

It is best to use an IDE like Pycharm to edit Python code as it provides development tools and built-in coding assistance. Code inspection makes coding and debugging faster and simpler, ensuring that you focus on the end goal of learning maths for neural networks.

The following steps show you how to set up local Python environment in Pycharm:

1. Go to **Preferences** and verify that the TensorFlow library is installed. If not, follow the instructions at `https://www.tensorflow.org/install/` to install TensorFlow:

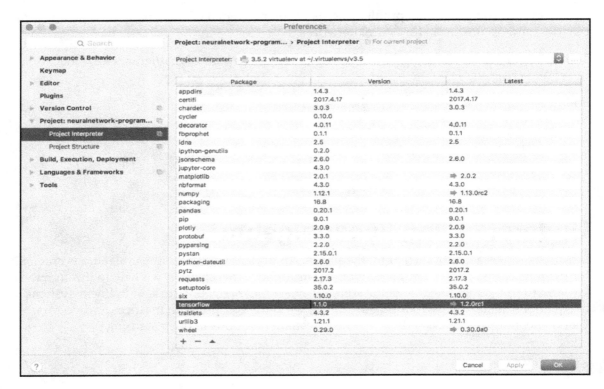

2. Keep the default options of TensorFlow and click on **OK**.
3. Finally, right-click on the source file and click on **Run 'matrices'**:

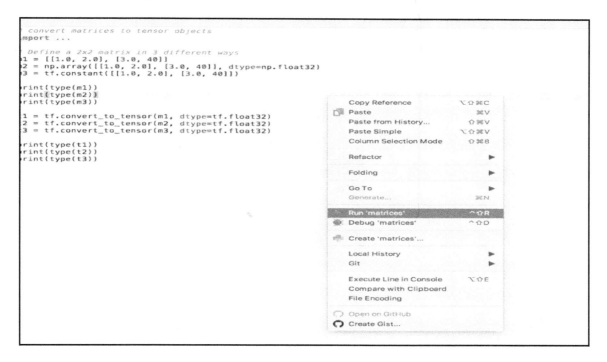

Linear algebra structures

In the following section, we will describe the fundamental structures of linear algebra.

Scalars, vectors, and matrices

Scalars, vectors, and matrices are the fundamental objects of mathematics. Basic definitions are listed as follows:

- Scalar is represented by a single number or numerical value called **magnitude**.
- Vector is an array of numbers assembled in order. A unique index identifies each number. Vector represents a point in space, with each element giving the coordinate along a different axis.
- Matrices is a two-dimensional array of numbers where each number is identified using two indices (i, j).

Tensors

An array of numbers with a variable number of axes is known as a **tensor**. For example, for three axes, it is identified using three indices (i, j, k).

The following image summaries a tensor, it describes a second-order tensor object. In a three-dimensional Cartesian coordinate system, tensor components will form the matrix:

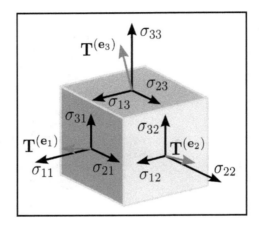

 Image reference is taken from tensor wiki `https://en.wikipedia.org/wiki/Tensor`

Operations

The following topics will describe the various operations of linear algebra.

Vectors

The Norm function is used to get the size of the vector; the norm of a vector x measures the distance from the origin to the point x. It is also known as the L^p norm, where $p=2$ is known as the **Euclidean norm**.

The following example shows you how to calculate the L^p norm of a given vector:

```
import tensorflow as tf

vector = tf.constant([[4,5,6]], dtype=tf.float32)
eucNorm = tf.norm(vector, ord="euclidean")

with tf.Session() as sess:
print(sess.run(eucNorm))
```

The output of the listing is 8.77496.

Matrices

A matrix is a two-dimensional array of numbers where each element is identified by two indices instead of just one. If a real matrix X has a height of m and a width of n, then we say that $X \in Rm \times n$. Here, R is a set of real numbers.

The following example shows how different matrices are converted to tensor objects:

```
# convert matrices to tensor objects
import numpy as np
import tensorflow as tf

# create a 2x2 matrix in various forms
matrix1 = [[1.0, 2.0], [3.0, 40]]
matrix2 = np.array([[1.0, 2.0], [3.0, 40]], dtype=np.float32)
matrix3 = tf.constant([[1.0, 2.0], [3.0, 40]])

print(type(matrix1))
print(type(matrix2))
print(type(matrix3))

tensorForM1 = tf.convert_to_tensor(matrix1, dtype=tf.float32)
tensorForM2 = tf.convert_to_tensor(matrix2, dtype=tf.float32)
tensorForM3 = tf.convert_to_tensor(matrix3, dtype=tf.float32)

print(type(tensorForM1))
print(type(tensorForM2))
print(type(tensorForM3))
```

The output of the listing is shown in the following code:

```
<class 'list'>
<class 'numpy.ndarray'>
<class 'tensorflow.python.framework.ops.Tensor'>
<class 'tensorflow.python.framework.ops.Tensor'>
<class 'tensorflow.python.framework.ops.Tensor'>
<class 'tensorflow.python.framework.ops.Tensor'>
```

Matrix multiplication

Matrix multiplication of matrices A and B is a third matrix, C:

$$C = AB$$

The element-wise product of matrices is called a **Hadamard** product and is denoted as $A.B$.

The dot product of two vectors x and y of the same dimensionality is the matrix product x transposing y. Matrix product $C = AB$ is like computing C_{ij} as the dot product between row i of matrix A and column j of matrix B:

$$C_{i,j} = \sum_{k} A_{i,k} B_{k,j}$$

The following example shows the Hadamard product and dot product using tensor objects:

```
import tensorflow as tf

mat1 = tf.constant([[4, 5, 6],[3,2,1]])
mat2 = tf.constant([[7, 8, 9],[10, 11, 12]])

# hadamard product (element wise)
mult = tf.multiply(mat1, mat2)

# dot product (no. of rows = no. of columns)
dotprod = tf.matmul(mat1, tf.transpose(mat2))

with tf.Session() as sess:
    print(sess.run(mult))
    print(sess.run(dotprod))
```

The output of the listing is shown as follows:

```
[[28 40 54][30 22 12]]
 [[122 167][ 46 64]]
```

Trace operator

The trace operator $Tr(A)$ of matrix A gives the sum of all of the diagonal entries of a matrix. The following example shows how to use a trace operator on tensor objects:

```
import tensorflow as tf

mat = tf.constant([
  [0, 1, 2],
  [3, 4, 5],
  [6, 7, 8]
], dtype=tf.float32)

  # get trace ('sum of diagonal elements') of the matrix
  mat = tf.trace(mat)

  with tf.Session() as sess:
    print(sess.run(mat))
```

The output of the listing is *12.0.*

Matrix transpose

Transposition of the matrix is the mirror image of the matrix across the main diagonal. A symmetric matrix is any matrix that is equal to its own transpose:

$$A = \begin{bmatrix} A_{1,1} & A_{1,2} \\ A_{2,1} & A_{2,2} \\ A_{3,1} & A_{3,2} \end{bmatrix} \Rightarrow A^{\mathrm{T}}$$

The following example shows how to use a transpose operator on tensor objects:

```
import tensorflow as tf

x = [[1,2,3],[4,5,6]]
x = tf.convert_to_tensor(x)
xtrans = tf.transpose(x)

y=([[[1,2,3],[6,5,4]],[[4,5,6],[3,6,3]]])
y = tf.convert_to_tensor(y)
ytrans = tf.transpose(y, perm=[0, 2, 1])

with tf.Session() as sess:
    print(sess.run(xtrans))
    print(sess.run(ytrans))
```

The output of the listing is shown as follows:

```
[[1 4] [2 5] [3 6]]
```

Matrix diagonals

Matrices that are diagonal in nature consist mostly of zeros and have non-zero entries only along the main diagonal. Not all diagonal matrices need to be square.

Using the diagonal part operation, we can get the diagonal of a given matrix, and to create a matrix with a given diagonal, we use the diag operation from tensorflow. The following example shows how to use diagonal operators on tensor objects:

```
import tensorflow as tf

mat = tf.constant([
  [0, 1, 2],
  [3, 4, 5],
  [6, 7, 8]
], dtype=tf.float32)

# get diagonal of the matrix
diag_mat = tf.diag_part(mat)

# create matrix with given diagonal
mat = tf.diag([1,2,3,4])

with tf.Session() as sess:
    print(sess.run(diag_mat))
    print(sess.run(mat))
```

The output of this is shown as follows:

```
[ 0.   4.   8.]
[[1 0 0 0] [0 2 0 0]  [0 0 3 0]  [0 0 0 4]]
```

Identity matrix

An identity matrix is a matrix I that does not change any vector, like V, when multiplied by I.

The following example shows how to get the identity matrix for a given size:

```
import tensorflow as tf

identity = tf.eye(3, 3)

with tf.Session() as sess:
    print(sess.run(identity))
```

The output of this is shown as follows:

```
[[ 1.   0.   0.] [ 0.   1.   0.] [ 0.   0.   1.]]
```

Inverse matrix

The matrix inverse of I is denoted as I^{-1}. Consider the following equation; to solve it using inverse and different values of b, there can be multiple solutions for x. Note the property:

$$A^{-1}A = 1$$
$$Ax = b$$
$$A^{-1}Ax = a^{-1b}$$
$$I_n x = A^{-1b}$$
$$x = A^{-1}b$$

The following example shows how to calculate the inverse of a matrix using the `matrix_inverse` operation:

```
import tensorflow as tf

mat = tf.constant([[2, 3, 4], [5, 6, 7], [8, 9, 10]], dtype=tf.float32)
print(mat)

inv_mat = tf.matrix_inverse(tf.transpose(mat))

with tf.Session() as sess:
print(sess.run(inv_mat))
```

Solving linear equations

TensorFlow can solve a series of linear equations using the `solve` operation. Let's first explain this without using the library and later use the `solve` function.

A linear equation is represented as follows:

$$ax + b = yy - ax = b$$

$$y - ax = b$$

$$y/b - a/b(x) = 1$$

Our job is to find the values for a and b in the preceding equation, given our observed points. First, create the matrix points. The first column represents x values, while the second column represents y values.
Consider that X is the input matrix and A is the parameters that we need to learn; we set up a system like $AX=B$, therefore, $A = BX^{-1}$.
The following example, with code, shows how to solve the linear equation:

$$3x+2y = 15$$
$$4x-y = 10$$

```
import tensorflow as tf

# equation 1
x1 = tf.constant(3, dtype=tf.float32)
y1 = tf.constant(2, dtype=tf.float32)
point1 = tf.stack([x1, y1])

# equation 2
```

```
x2 = tf.constant(4, dtype=tf.float32)
y2 = tf.constant(-1, dtype=tf.float32)
point2 = tf.stack([x2, y2])

# solve for AX=C
X = tf.transpose(tf.stack([point1, point2]))
C = tf.ones((1,2), dtype=tf.float32)

A = tf.matmul(C, tf.matrix_inverse(X))

with tf.Session() as sess:
    X = sess.run(X)
    print(X)

    A = sess.run(A)
    print(A)

b = 1 / A[0][1]
a = -b * A[0][0]
print("Hence Linear Equation is: y = {a}x + {b}".format(a=a, b=b))
```

The output of the listing is shown as follows:

```
[[ 3. 4.][ 2. -1.]]
 [[ 0.27272728 0.09090909]]
Hence Linear Equation is: y = -2.999999999999996x + 10.999999672174463
```

The canonical equation for a circle is $x2+y2+dx+ey+f=0$; to solve this for the parameters *d*, *e*, and *f*, we use TensorFlow's solve operation as follows:

```
# canonical circle equation
# x2+y2+dx+ey+f = 0
# dx+ey+f=-(x2+y2) ==> AX = B
# we have to solve for d, e, f

points = tf.constant([[2,1], [0,5], [-1,2]], dtype=tf.float64)
X = tf.constant([[2,1,1], [0,5,1], [-1,2,1]], dtype=tf.float64)
B = -tf.constant([[5], [25], [5]], dtype=tf.float64)

A = tf.matrix_solve(X,B)

with tf.Session() as sess:
    result = sess.run(A)
    D, E, F = result.flatten()
    print("Hence Circle Equation is: x**2 + y**2 + {D}x + {E}y + {F} =
0".format(**locals()))
```

The output of the listing is shown in the following code:

```
Hence Circle Equation is: x**2 + y**2 + -2.0x + -6.0y + 5.0 = 0
```

Singular value decomposition

When we decompose an integer into its prime factors, we can understand useful properties about the integer. Similarly, when we decompose a matrix, we can understand many functional properties that are not directly evident. There are two types of decomposition, namely eigenvalue decomposition and singular value decomposition.

All real matrices have singular value decomposition, but the same is not true for Eigenvalue decomposition. For example, if a matrix is not square, the Eigen decomposition is not defined and we must use singular value decomposition instead.

Singular Value Decomposition (SVD) in mathematical form is the product of three matrices U, S, and V, where U is $m*r$, S is $r*r$ and V is $r*n$:

$$A_{m \times n} = USV^{-1}$$

The following example shows SVD using a TensorFlow svd operation on textual data:

```
import numpy as np
import tensorflow as tf
import matplotlib.pyplot as plts

path = "/neuralnetwork-programming/ch01/plots"

text = ["I", "like", "enjoy",
        "deep", "learning", "NLP", "flying", "."]
xMatrix = np.array([[0,2,1,0,0,0,0,0],
              [2,0,0,1,0,1,0,0],
              [1,0,0,0,0,0,1,0],
              [0,1,0,0,1,0,0,0],
              [0,0,0,1,0,0,0,1],
              [0,1,0,0,0,0,0,1],
              [0,0,1,0,0,0,0,1],
              [0,0,0,0,1,1,1,0]], dtype=np.float32)

X_tensor = tf.convert_to_tensor(xMatrix, dtype=tf.float32)

# tensorflow svd
with tf.Session() as sess:
    s, U, Vh = sess.run(tf.svd(X_tensor, full_matrices=False))
```

```
for i in range(len(text)):
    plts.text(U[i,0], U[i,1], text[i])

plts.ylim(-0.8,0.8)
plts.xlim(-0.8,2.0)
plts.savefig(path + '/svd_tf.png')

# numpy svd
la = np.linalg
U, s, Vh = la.svd(xMatrix, full_matrices=False)

print(U)
print(s)
print(Vh)

# write matrices to file (understand concepts)
file = open(path + "/matx.txt", 'w')
file.write(str(U))
file.write("\n")
file.write("=============")
file.write("\n")
file.write(str(s))
file.close()

for i in range(len(text)):
    plts.text(U[i,0], U[i,1], text[i])

plts.ylim(-0.8,0.8)
plts.xlim(-0.8,2.0)
plts.savefig(path + '/svd_np.png')
```

The output of this is shown as follows:

```
[[ -5.24124920e-01   -5.72859168e-01    9.54463035e-02    3.83228481e-01
  -1.76963374e-01   -1.76092178e-01   -4.19185609e-01   -5.57702743e-02]
 [ -5.94438076e-01    6.30120635e-01   -1.70207784e-01    3.10038358e-0
   1.84062332e-01   -2.34777853e-01    1.29535481e-01    1.36813134e-01]
 [ -2.56274015e-01    2.74017543e-01    1.59810841e-01    3.73903001e-16
  -5.78984618e-01    6.36550903e-01   -3.32297325e-16   -3.05414885e-01]
 [ -2.85637408e-01   -2.47912124e-01    3.54610324e-01   -7.31901303e-02
   4.45784479e-01    8.36141407e-02    5.48721075e-01   -4.68012422e-01]
 [ -1.93139315e-01    3.38495038e-02   -5.00790417e-01   -4.28462476e-01
   3.47110212e-01    1.55483231e-01   -4.68663752e-01   -4.03576553e-01]
 [ -3.05134684e-01   -2.93989003e-01   -2.23433599e-01   -1.91614240e-01
   1.27460942e-01    4.91219401e-01    2.09592804e-01    6.57535374e-01]
 [ -1.82489842e-01   -1.61027774e-01   -3.97842437e-01   -3.83228481e-01
  -5.12923241e-01   -4.27574426e-01    4.19185609e-01   -1.18313827e-01]
 [ -2.46898428e-01    1.57254755e-01    5.92991650e-01   -6.20076716e-01
```

```
    -3.21868137e-02   -2.31065080e-01   -2.59070963e-01    2.37976909e-01]]
 [ 2.75726271  2.67824793  1.89221275  1.61803401  1.19154561  0.94833982
   0.61803401  0.56999218]
 [[ -5.24124920e-01   -5.94438076e-01   -2.56274015e-01   -2.85637408e-01
    -1.93139315e-01   -3.05134684e-01   -1.82489842e-01   -2.46898428e-01]
  [  5.72859168e-01   -6.30120635e-01   -2.74017543e-01    2.47912124e-01
    -3.38495038e-02    2.93989003e-01    1.61027774e-01   -1.57254755e-01]
  [ -9.54463035e-02    1.70207784e-01   -1.59810841e-01   -3.54610324e-01
     5.00790417e-01    2.23433599e-01    3.97842437e-01   -5.92991650e-01]
  [  3.83228481e-01    3.10038358e-01   -2.22044605e-16   -7.31901303e-02
    -4.28462476e-01   -1.91614240e-01   -3.83228481e-01   -6.20076716e-01]
  [ -1.76963374e-01    1.84062332e-01   -5.78984618e-01    4.45784479e-01
     3.47110212e-01    1.27460942e-01   -5.12923241e-01   -3.21868137e-02]
  [  1.76092178e-01    2.34777853e-01   -6.36550903e-01   -8.36141407e-02
    -1.55483231e-01   -4.91219401e-01    4.27574426e-01    2.31065080e-01]
  [  4.19185609e-01   -1.29535481e-01   -3.33066907e-16   -5.48721075e-01
     4.68663752e-01   -2.09592804e-01   -4.19185609e-01    2.59070963e-01]
  [ -5.57702743e-02    1.36813134e-01   -3.05414885e-01   -4.68012422e-01
    -4.03576553e-01    6.57535374e-01   -1.18313827e-01    2.37976909e-01]]
```

Here is the plot for the SVD of the preceding dataset:

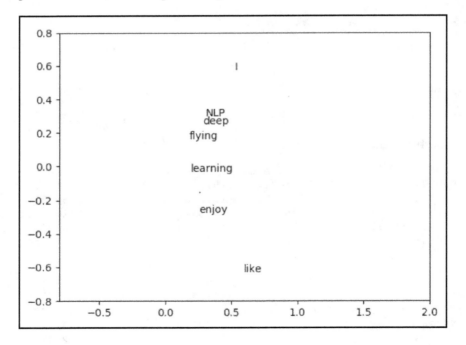

Eigenvalue decomposition

Eigen decomposition is one of the most famous decomposition techniques in which we decompose a matrix into a set of eigenvectors and eigenvalues.

For a square matrix, Eigenvector is a vector v such that multiplication by A alters only the scale of v:

$$Av = \lambda v$$

The scalar λ is known as the eigenvalue corresponding to this eigenvector.

Eigen decomposition of A is then given as follows:

$$A = Vdiag\left(\lambda\right)V^{-1}$$

Eigen decomposition of a matrix describes many useful details about the matrix. For example, the matrix is singular if, and only if, any of the eigenvalues are zero.

Principal Component Analysis

Principal Component Analysis (PCA) projects the given dataset onto a lower dimensional linear space so that the variance of the projected data is maximized. PCA requires the eigenvalues and eigenvectors of the covariance matrix, which is the product where X is the data matrix.

SVD on the data matrix X is given as follows:

$$X = U \Sigma V^{T}$$

$$XX^{T} = \left(U \Sigma V^{T}\right)\left(U \Sigma V^{T}\right)^{T}$$
$$XX^{T} = \left(U \Sigma V^{T}\right)\left(V \Sigma U^{T}\right)$$

$$XX^{T} = U \Sigma^{2} U^{T}$$

The following example shows PCA using SVD:

```
import numpy as np
import tensorflow as tf
import matplotlib.pyplot as plt
import plotly.plotly as py
import plotly.graph_objs as go
import plotly.figure_factory as FF
import pandas as pd

path = "/neuralnetwork-programming/ch01/plots"
logs = "/neuralnetwork-programming/ch01/logs"

xMatrix = np.array([[0,2,1,0,0,0,0,0],
            [2,0,0,1,0,1,0,0],
            [1,0,0,0,0,0,1,0],
            [0,1,0,0,1,0,0,0],
            [0,0,0,1,0,0,0,1],
            [0,1,0,0,0,0,0,1],
            [0,0,1,0,0,0,0,1],
            [0,0,0,0,1,1,1,0]], dtype=np.float32)

def pca(mat):
    mat = tf.constant(mat, dtype=tf.float32)
    mean = tf.reduce_mean(mat, 0)
    less = mat - mean
    s, u, v = tf.svd(less, full_matrices=True, compute_uv=True)

    s2 = s ** 2
    variance_ratio = s2 / tf.reduce_sum(s2)

    with tf.Session() as session:
        run = session.run([variance_ratio])
    return run


if __name__ == '__main__':
    print(pca(xMatrix))
```

The output of the listing is shown as follows:

```
[array([  4.15949494e-01,    2.08390564e-01,    1.90929279e-01,
          8.36438537e-02,    5.55494241e-02,    2.46047471e-02,
          2.09326427e-02,    3.57540098e-16], dtype=float32)]
```

Calculus

Topics in the previous sections are covered as part of standard linear algebra; something that wasn't covered is basic calculus. Despite the fact that the calculus that we use is relatively simple, the mathematical form of it may look very complex. In this section, we present some basic forms of matrix calculus with a few examples.

Gradient

Gradient for functions with respect to a real-valued matrix A is defined as the matrix of partial derivatives of A and is denoted as follows:

$$\nabla_A f(A) \in \mathbb{R}^{m \times n} = \begin{bmatrix} \dfrac{\partial f(A)}{\partial A_{11}} & \dfrac{\partial f(A)}{\partial A_{12}} & \cdots & \dfrac{\partial f(A)}{\partial A_{1n}} \\ \dfrac{\partial f(A)}{\partial A_{21}} & \dfrac{\partial f(A)}{\partial A_{22}} & \cdots & \dfrac{\partial f(A)}{\partial A_{2n}} \\ \vdots & \vdots & \ddots & \vdots \\ \dfrac{\partial f(A)}{\partial A_{m1}} & \dfrac{\partial f(A)}{\partial A_{m2}} & \cdots & \dfrac{\partial f(A)}{\partial A_{mn}} \end{bmatrix}$$

$$\left(\nabla_A f(A)\right)ij = \frac{\partial f(A)}{\partial A_{ij}}$$

TensorFlow does not do numerical differentiation; rather, it supports automatic differentiation. By specifying operations in a TensorFlow graph, it can automatically run the chain rule through the graph and, as it knows the derivatives of each operation we specify, it can combine them automatically.

The following example shows training a network using MNIST data, the MNIST database consists of handwritten digits. It has a training set of 60,000 examples and a test set of 10,000 samples. The digits are size-normalized.

Here backpropagation is performed without any API usage and derivatives are calculated manually. We get 913 correct out of 1,000 tests. This concept will be introduced in the next chapter.

The following code snippet describes how to get the `mnist` dataset and initialize weights and biases:

```
import tensorflow as tf

# get mnist dataset
from tensorflow.examples.tutorials.mnist import input_data
data = input_data.read_data_sets("MNIST_data/", one_hot=True)

# x represents image with 784 values as columns (28*28), y represents
output digit
x = tf.placeholder(tf.float32, [None, 784])
y = tf.placeholder(tf.float32, [None, 10])

# initialize weights and biases [w1,b1][w2,b2]
numNeuronsInDeepLayer = 30
w1 = tf.Variable(tf.truncated_normal([784, numNeuronsInDeepLayer]))
b1 = tf.Variable(tf.truncated_normal([1, numNeuronsInDeepLayer]))
w2 = tf.Variable(tf.truncated_normal([numNeuronsInDeepLayer, 10]))
b2 = tf.Variable(tf.truncated_normal([1, 10]))
```

We now define a two-layered network with a nonlinear `sigmoid` function; a squared loss function is applied and optimized using a backward propagation algorithm, as shown in the following snippet:

```
# non-linear sigmoid function at each neuron
def sigmoid(x):
    sigma = tf.div(tf.constant(1.0), tf.add(tf.constant(1.0),
tf.exp(tf.negative(x))))
    return sigma

# starting from first layer with wx+b, then apply sigmoid to add non-
linearity
z1 = tf.add(tf.matmul(x, w1), b1)
a1 = sigmoid(z1)
z2 = tf.add(tf.matmul(a1, w2), b2)
a2 = sigmoid(z2)

# calculate the loss (delta)
loss = tf.subtract(a2, y)

# derivative of the sigmoid function der(sigmoid)=sigmoid*(1-sigmoid)
def sigmaprime(x):
    return tf.multiply(sigmoid(x), tf.subtract(tf.constant(1.0),
sigmoid(x)))

# backward propagation
dz2 = tf.multiply(loss, sigmaprime(z2))
```

```
db2 = dz2
dw2 = tf.matmul(tf.transpose(a1), dz2)

da1 = tf.matmul(dz2, tf.transpose(w2))
dz1 = tf.multiply(da1, sigmaprime(z1))
db1 = dz1
dw1 = tf.matmul(tf.transpose(x), dz1)

# finally update the network
eta = tf.constant(0.5)
step = [
    tf.assign(w1,
            tf.subtract(w1, tf.multiply(eta, dw1)))
    , tf.assign(b1,
            tf.subtract(b1, tf.multiply(eta,
                                    tf.reduce_mean(db1,
axis=[0])))))
    , tf.assign(w2,
            tf.subtract(w2, tf.multiply(eta, dw2)))
    , tf.assign(b2,
            tf.subtract(b2, tf.multiply(eta,
                                    tf.reduce_mean(db2,
axis=[0])))))
]

acct_mat = tf.equal(tf.argmax(a2, 1), tf.argmax(y, 1))
acct_res = tf.reduce_sum(tf.cast(acct_mat, tf.float32))

sess = tf.InteractiveSession()
sess.run(tf.global_variables_initializer())

for i in range(10000):
    batch_xs, batch_ys = data.train.next_batch(10)
    sess.run(step, feed_dict={x: batch_xs,
                                y: batch_ys})
    if i % 1000 == 0:
        res = sess.run(acct_res, feed_dict=
        {x: data.test.images[:1000],
         y: data.test.labels[:1000]})
        print(res)
```

The output of this is shown as follows:

```
Extracting MNIST_data
125.0
814.0
870.0
874.0
```

```
889.0
897.0
906.0
903.0
922.0
913.0
```

Now, let's use automatic differentiation with TensorFlow. The following example demonstrates the use of `GradientDescentOptimizer`. We get 924 correct out of 1,000 tests.

```python
import tensorflow as tf

# get mnist dataset
from tensorflow.examples.tutorials.mnist import input_data
data = input_data.read_data_sets("MNIST_data/", one_hot=True)

# x represents image with 784 values as columns (28*28), y represents
output digit
x = tf.placeholder(tf.float32, [None, 784])
y = tf.placeholder(tf.float32, [None, 10])

# initialize weights and biases [w1,b1][w2,b2]
numNeuronsInDeepLayer = 30
w1 = tf.Variable(tf.truncated_normal([784, numNeuronsInDeepLayer]))
b1 = tf.Variable(tf.truncated_normal([1, numNeuronsInDeepLayer]))
w2 = tf.Variable(tf.truncated_normal([numNeuronsInDeepLayer, 10]))
b2 = tf.Variable(tf.truncated_normal([1, 10]))

# non-linear sigmoid function at each neuron
def sigmoid(x):
    sigma = tf.div(tf.constant(1.0), tf.add(tf.constant(1.0),
tf.exp(tf.negative(x))))
    return sigma

# starting from first layer with wx+b, then apply sigmoid to add non-
linearity
z1 = tf.add(tf.matmul(x, w1), b1)
a1 = sigmoid(z1)
z2 = tf.add(tf.matmul(a1, w2), b2)
a2 = sigmoid(z2)

# calculate the loss (delta)
loss = tf.subtract(a2, y)

# derivative of the sigmoid function der(sigmoid)=sigmoid*(1-sigmoid)
def sigmaprime(x):
    return tf.multiply(sigmoid(x), tf.subtract(tf.constant(1.0),
```

```
sigmoid(x)))

# automatic differentiation
cost = tf.multiply(loss, loss)
step = tf.train.GradientDescentOptimizer(0.1).minimize(cost)

acct_mat = tf.equal(tf.argmax(a2, 1), tf.argmax(y, 1))
acct_res = tf.reduce_sum(tf.cast(acct_mat, tf.float32))

sess = tf.InteractiveSession()
sess.run(tf.global_variables_initializer())

for i in range(10000):
    batch_xs, batch_ys = data.train.next_batch(10)
    sess.run(step, feed_dict={x: batch_xs,
                              y: batch_ys})
    if i % 1000 == 0:
        res = sess.run(acct_res, feed_dict=
        {x: data.test.images[:1000],
         y: data.test.labels[:1000]})
        print(res)
```

The output of this is shown as follows:

```
96.0
777.0
862.0
870.0
889.0
901.0
911.0
905.0
914.0
924.0
```

The following example shows linear regression using gradient descent:

```
import tensorflow as tf
import numpy
import matplotlib.pyplot as plt
rndm = numpy.random

# config parameters
learningRate = 0.01
trainingEpochs = 1000
displayStep = 50

# create the training data
```

```
trainX = numpy.asarray([3.3,4.4,5.5,6.71,6.93,4.168,9.779,6.182,7.59,2.167,
                        7.042,10.791,5.313,7.997,5.654,9.27,3.12])
trainY =
numpy.asarray([1.7,2.76,2.09,3.19,1.694,1.573,3.366,2.596,2.53,1.221,
                        2.827,3.465,1.65,2.904,2.42,2.94,1.34])
nSamples = trainX.shape[0]

# tf inputs
X = tf.placeholder("float")
Y = tf.placeholder("float")

# initialize weights and bias
W = tf.Variable(rndm.randn(), name="weight")
b = tf.Variable(rndm.randn(), name="bias")

# linear model
linearModel = tf.add(tf.multiply(X, W), b)

# mean squared error
loss = tf.reduce_sum(tf.pow(linearModel-Y, 2))/(2*nSamples)

# Gradient descent
opt = tf.train.GradientDescentOptimizer(learningRate).minimize(loss)

# initializing variables
init = tf.global_variables_initializer()

# run
with tf.Session() as sess:
    sess.run(init)

    # fitting the training data
    for epoch in range(trainingEpochs):
        for (x, y) in zip(trainX, trainY):
            sess.run(opt, feed_dict={X: x, Y: y})

        # print logs
        if (epoch+1) % displayStep == 0:
            c = sess.run(loss, feed_dict={X: trainX, Y:trainY})
            print("Epoch is:", '%04d' % (epoch+1), "loss=",
"{:.9f}".format(c), "W=", sess.run(W), "b=", sess.run(b))

    print("optimization done...")
    trainingLoss = sess.run(loss, feed_dict={X: trainX, Y: trainY})
    print("Training loss=", trainingLoss, "W=", sess.run(W), "b=",
sess.run(b), '\n')

    # display the plot
```

```
    plt.plot(trainX, trainY, 'ro', label='Original data')
    plt.plot(trainX, sess.run(W) * trainX + sess.run(b), label='Fitted
line')
    plt.legend()
    plt.show()

    # Testing example, as requested (Issue #2)
    testX = numpy.asarray([6.83, 4.668, 8.9, 7.91, 5.7, 8.7, 3.1, 2.1])
    testY = numpy.asarray([1.84, 2.273, 3.2, 2.831, 2.92, 3.24, 1.35,
1.03])

    print("Testing... (Mean square loss Comparison)")
    testing_cost = sess.run(
        tf.reduce_sum(tf.pow(linearModel - Y, 2)) / (2 * testX.shape[0]),
        feed_dict={X: testX, Y: testY})
    print("Testing cost=", testing_cost)
    print("Absolute mean square loss difference:", abs(trainingLoss -
testing_cost))

    plt.plot(testX, testY, 'bo', label='Testing data')
    plt.plot(trainX, sess.run(W) * trainX + sess.run(b), label='Fitted
line')
    plt.legend()
    plt.show()
```

The output of this is shown as follows:

```
Epoch is: 0050 loss= 0.141912043 W= 0.10565 b= 1.8382
 Epoch is: 0100 loss= 0.134377643 W= 0.11413 b= 1.7772
 Epoch is: 0150 loss= 0.127711013 W= 0.122106 b= 1.71982
 Epoch is: 0200 loss= 0.121811897 W= 0.129609 b= 1.66585
 Epoch is: 0250 loss= 0.116592340 W= 0.136666 b= 1.61508
 Epoch is: 0300 loss= 0.111973859 W= 0.143304 b= 1.56733
 Epoch is: 0350 loss= 0.107887231 W= 0.149547 b= 1.52241
 Epoch is: 0400 loss= 0.104270980 W= 0.15542 b= 1.48017
 Epoch is: 0450 loss= 0.101070963 W= 0.160945 b= 1.44043
 Epoch is: 0500 loss= 0.098239250 W= 0.166141 b= 1.40305
 Epoch is: 0550 loss= 0.095733419 W= 0.171029 b= 1.36789
 Epoch is: 0600 loss= 0.093516059 W= 0.175626 b= 1.33481
 Epoch is: 0650 loss= 0.091553882 W= 0.179951 b= 1.3037
 Epoch is: 0700 loss= 0.089817807 W= 0.184018 b= 1.27445
 Epoch is: 0750 loss= 0.088281371 W= 0.187843 b= 1.24692
 Epoch is: 0800 loss= 0.086921677 W= 0.191442 b= 1.22104
 Epoch is: 0850 loss= 0.085718453 W= 0.194827 b= 1.19669
 Epoch is: 0900 loss= 0.084653646 W= 0.198011 b= 1.17378
 Epoch is: 0950 loss= 0.083711281 W= 0.201005 b= 1.15224
 Epoch is: 1000 loss= 0.082877308 W= 0.203822 b= 1.13198
 optimization done...
```

```
Training loss= 0.0828773 W= 0.203822 b= 1.13198
Testing... (Mean square loss Comparison)
Testing cost= 0.0957726
Absolute mean square loss difference: 0.0128952
```

The plots are as follows:

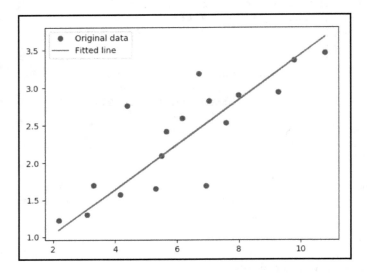

The following image shows the fitted line on testing data using the model:

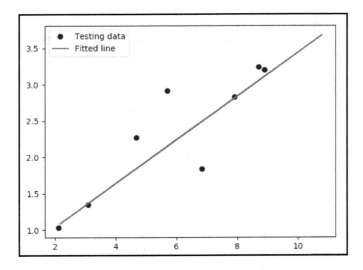

Hessian

Gradient is the first derivative for functions of vectors, whereas hessian is the second derivative. We will go through the notation now:

$$
\nabla_{x}^{2}f\left(x\right)\in\mathbb{R}^{n\times m}=
\begin{bmatrix}
\dfrac{\partial^{2}f\left(x\right)}{\partial x_{1}^{2}} & \dfrac{\partial^{2}f\left(x\right)}{\partial x_{1}\partial x_{2}} & \cdots & \dfrac{\partial^{2}f\left(x\right)}{\partial x_{1}\partial x_{n}} \\[2ex]
\dfrac{\partial^{2}f\left(x\right)}{\partial x_{2}\partial x_{1}} & \dfrac{\partial^{2}f\left(x\right)}{\partial x_{2}^{2}} & \cdots & \dfrac{\partial^{2}f\left(x\right)}{\partial x_{2}\partial x_{n}} \\[2ex]
\vdots & \vdots & \ddots & \vdots \\[2ex]
\dfrac{\partial^{2}f\left(x\right)}{\partial x_{n}\partial x_{1}} & \dfrac{\partial^{2}f\left(x\right)}{\partial x_{n}\partial x_{2}} & \cdots & \dfrac{\partial^{2}f\left(x\right)}{\partial x_{n}^{2}}
\end{bmatrix}
$$

Similar to the gradient, the hessian is defined only when $f(x)$ is real-valued.

The algebraic function used is
$$q\left(x\right)=x_{1}^{2}+2x_{1}x_{2}+3x_{2}^{2}+4x_{1}+5x_{2}+6$$.

The following example shows the hessian implementation using TensorFlow:

```
import tensorflow as tf
import numpy as np

X = tf.Variable(np.random.random_sample(), dtype=tf.float32)
y = tf.Variable(np.random.random_sample(), dtype=tf.float32)

def createCons(x):
    return tf.constant(x, dtype=tf.float32)

function = tf.pow(X, createCons(2)) + createCons(2) * X * y + createCons(3)
* tf.pow(y, createCons(2)) + createCons(4) * X + createCons(5) * y +
createCons(6)

# compute hessian
def hessian(func, varbles):
    matrix = []
    for v_1 in varbles:
        tmp = []
        for v_2 in varbles:
```

```
            # calculate derivative twice, first w.r.t v2 and then w.r.t v1
            tmp.append(tf.gradients(tf.gradients(func, v_2)[0], v_1)[0])
        tmp = [createCons(0) if t == None else t for t in tmp]
        tmp = tf.stack(tmp)
        matrix.append(tmp)
    matrix = tf.stack(matrix)
    return matrix

hessian = hessian(function, [X, y])

sess = tf.Session()
sess.run(tf.initialize_all_variables())
print(sess.run(hessian))
```

The output of this is shown as follows:

```
[[ 2.   2.] [ 2.   6.]]
```

Determinant

Determinant shows us information about the matrix that is helpful in linear equations and also helps in finding the inverse of a matrix.

For a given matrix X, the determinant is shown as follows:

$$X = \begin{matrix} a & b & c \\ d & e & f \\ g & h & i \end{matrix}$$

$$\det(X) = a(ei - fh) - b(di - fg) - c(dh - eg)$$

The following example shows how to get a determinant using TensorFlow:

```
import tensorflow as tf
import numpy as np

x = np.array([[10.0, 15.0, 20.0], [0.0, 1.0, 5.0], [3.0, 5.0, 7.0]],
dtype=np.float32)

det = tf.matrix_determinant(x)

with tf.Session() as sess:
    print(sess.run(det))
```

The output of this is shown as follows:

```
-15.0
```

Optimization

As part of deep learning, we mostly would like to optimize the value of a function that either minimizes or maximizes *f(x)* with respect to *x*. A few examples of optimization problems are least-squares, logistic regression, and support vector machines. Many of these techniques will get examined in detail in later chapters.

Optimizers

We will study `AdamOptimizer` here; TensorFlow `AdamOptimizer` uses Kingma and Ba's Adam algorithm to manage the learning rate. Adam has many advantages over the simple `GradientDescentOptimizer`. The first is that it uses moving averages of the parameters, which enables Adam to use a larger step size, and it will converge to this step size without any fine-tuning.

The disadvantage of Adam is that it requires more computation to be performed for each parameter in each training step. `GradientDescentOptimizer` can be used as well, but it would require more hyperparameter tuning before it would converge as quickly.
The following example shows how to use `AdamOptimizer`:

- `tf.train.Optimizer` creates an optimizer
- `tf.train.Optimizer.minimize(loss, var_list)` adds the optimization operation to the computation graph

Here, automatic differentiation computes gradients without user input:

```
import numpy as np
import seaborn
import matplotlib.pyplot as plt
import tensorflow as tf

# input dataset
xData = np.arange(100, step=.1)
yData = xData + 20 * np.sin(xData/10)

# scatter plot for input data
plt.scatter(xData, yData)
plt.show()
```

```
# defining data size and batch size
nSamples = 1000
batchSize = 100

# resize
xData = np.reshape(xData, (nSamples,1))
yData = np.reshape(yData, (nSamples,1))

# input placeholders
x = tf.placeholder(tf.float32, shape=(batchSize, 1))
y = tf.placeholder(tf.float32, shape=(batchSize, 1))

# init weight and bias
with tf.variable_scope("linearRegression"):
 W = tf.get_variable("weights", (1, 1),
initializer=tf.random_normal_initializer())
 b = tf.get_variable("bias", (1,),
initializer=tf.constant_initializer(0.0))

 y_pred = tf.matmul(x, W) + b
 loss = tf.reduce_sum((y - y_pred)**2/nSamples)

# optimizer
opt = tf.train.AdamOptimizer().minimize(loss)
with tf.Session() as sess:
    sess.run(tf.global_variables_initializer())

    # gradient descent loop for 500 steps
    for _ in range(500):
     # random minibatch
     indices = np.random.choice(nSamples, batchSize)

    X_batch, y_batch = xData[indices], yData[indices]

    # gradient descent step
    _, loss_val = sess.run([opt, loss], feed_dict={x: X_batch, y:
y_batch})
```

Here is the scatter plot for the dataset:

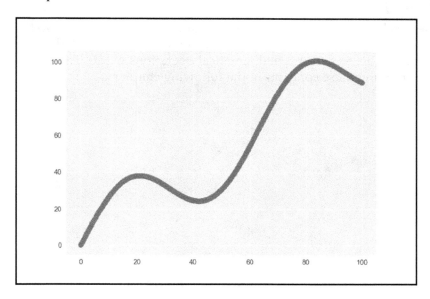

This is the plot of the learned model on the data:

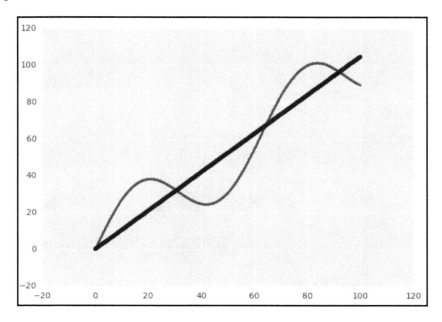

Summary

In this chapter, we've introduced the mathematical concepts that are key to the understanding of neural networks and reviewed some maths associated with tensors. We also demonstrated how to perform mathematical operations within TensorFlow. We will repeatedly be applying these concepts in the following chapters.

2
Deep Feedforward Networks

In the first chapter, you learned about the mathematics which drives the logic behind all kinds of neural networks. In this chapter, we are going to focus on the most fundamental neutral networks, which are called **feedforward neural networks**. We will also look at deep feedforward networks with multiple hidden layers to improve the accuracy of the model.

We will be covering the following topics:

- Defining feedforward networks
- Understanding backpropagation
- Implementing feedforward networks in TensorFlow
- Analyzing the Iris dataset
- Creating feedforward networks for image classification

Defining feedforward networks

Deep feedforward networks, also called feedforward neural networks, are sometimes also referred to as **Multilayer Perceptrons (MLPs)**. The goal of a feedforward network is to approximate the function of $f*$. For example, for a classifier, $y=f*(x)$ maps an input x to a label y. A feedforward network defines a mapping from input to label $y=f(x;\theta)$. It learns the value of the parameter θ that results in the best function approximation.

We discuss RNNs in Chapter 5, *Recurrent Neural Networks*. Feedforward networks are a conceptual stepping stone on the path to recurrent networks, which power many natural language applications. Feedforward neural networks are called networks because they compose together many different functions which represent them. These functions are composed in a directed acyclic graph.

The model is associated with a directed acyclic graph describing how the functions are composed together. For example, there are three functions *f(1)*, *f(2)*, and *f(3)* connected to form *f(x) =f(3)(f(2)(f(1)(x)))*. These chain structures are the most commonly used structures of neural networks. In this case, *f(1)* is called the **first layer** of the network, *f(2)* is called the **second layer**, and so on. The overall length of the chain gives the depth of the model. It is from this terminology that the name deep learning arises. The final layer of a feedforward network is called the **output layer**.

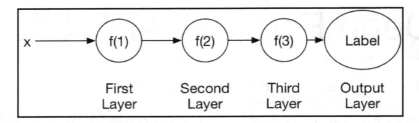

Diagram showing various functions activated on input x to form a neural network

These networks are called neural because they are inspired by neuroscience. Each hidden layer is a vector. The dimensionality of these hidden layers determines the width of the model.

Understanding backpropagation

When a feedforward neural network is used to accept an input x and produce an output $\hat{y}$, information flows forward through the network elements. The input x provides the information that then propagates up to the hidden units at each layer and produces $\hat{y}$. This is called **forward propagation**. During training, forward propagation continues onward until it produces a scalar cost $J(\theta)$. The backpropagation algorithm, often called backprop, allows the information from the cost to then flow backward through the network in order to compute the gradient.

Computing an analytical expression for the gradient is straightforward, but numerically evaluating such an expression can be computationally expensive. The backpropagation algorithm does so using a simple and inexpensive procedure.

> Backpropagation refers only to the method to compute the gradient, while another algorithm, such as stochastic gradient descent, refers to the actual mechanism.

Implementing feedforward networks with TensorFlow

Feedforward networks can be easily implemented using TensorFlow by defining placeholders for hidden layers, computing the activation values, and using them to calculate predictions. Let's take an example of classification with a feedforward network:

```
X = tf.placeholder("float", shape=[None, x_size])
y = tf.placeholder("float", shape=[None, y_size])
weights_1 = initialize_weights((x_size, hidden_size), stddev)
weights_2 = initialize_weights((hidden_size, y_size), stddev)
sigmoid = tf.nn.sigmoid(tf.matmul(X, weights_1))
y = tf.matmul(sigmoid, weights_2)
```

Once the predicted value tensor has been defined, we calculate the cost function:

```
cost = tf.reduce_mean(tf.nn.OPERATION_NAME(labels=<actual value>,
logits=<predicted value>))
updates_sgd = tf.train.GradientDescentOptimizer(sgd_step).minimize(cost)
```

Here, OPERATION_NAME could be one of the following:

- tf.nn.sigmoid_cross_entropy_with_logits: Calculates sigmoid cross entropy on incoming logits and labels:

```
sigmoid_cross_entropy_with_logits(
  _sentinel=None,
  labels=None,
  logits=None,
  name=None
)Formula implemented is max(x, 0) - x * z + log(1 + exp(-abs(x)))
```

_sentinel: Used to prevent positional parameters. Internal, do not use.
labels: A tensor of the same type and shape as logits.
logits: A tensor of type float32 or float64. The formula implemented is ($x = logits, z = labels$) max(x, 0) - x * z + log(1 + exp(-abs(x))).

- tf.nn.softmax: Performs softmax activation on the incoming tensor. This only normalizes to make sure all the probabilities in a tensor row add up to one. It cannot be directly used in a classification.

```
softmax = exp(logits) / reduce_sum(exp(logits), dim)
```

`logits`: A non-empty tensor. Must be one of the following types--half, `float32`, or `float64`.

`dim`: The dimension `softmax` will be performed on. The default is -1, which indicates the last dimension.

`name`: A name for the operation (optional).

`tf.nn.log_softmax`: Calculates the log of the `softmax` function and helps in normalizing underfitting. This function is also just a normalization function.

```
log_softmax(
  logits,
  dim=-1,
  name=None
)
```

`logits`: A non-empty tensor. Must be one of the following types--half, `float32`, or `float64`.

`dim`: The dimension `softmax` will be performed on. The default is -1, which indicates the last dimension.

`name`: A name for the operation (optional).

- `tf.nn.softmax_cross_entropy_with_logits`

```
softmax_cross_entropy_with_logits(
  _sentinel=None,
  labels=None,
  logits=None,
  dim=-1,
  name=None
)
```

`_sentinel`: Used to prevent positional parameters. For internal use only.

`labels`: Each rows `labels[i]` must be a valid probability distribution.

`logits`: Unscaled log probabilities.

`dim`: The class dimension. Defaulted to -1, which is the last dimension.

`name`: A name for the operation (optional).

The preceding code snippet computes `softmax` cross entropy between `logits` and `labels`. While the classes are mutually exclusive, their probabilities need not be. All that is required is that each row of labels is a valid probability distribution. For exclusive labels, use (where one and only one class is true at a time) `sparse_softmax_cross_entropy_with_logits`.

- `tf.nn.sparse_softmax_cross_entropy_with_logits`

```
sparse_softmax_cross_entropy_with_logits(
  _sentinel=None,
  labels=None,
  logits=None,
  name=None
)
```

`labels`: Tensor of shape [d_0, d_1, ..., $d\_(r-1)$] (where r is the rank of labels and result) and `dtype`, `int32`, or `int64`. Each entry in labels must be an index in [0, `num_classes`). Other values will raise an exception when this operation is run on the CPU and return NaN for corresponding loss and gradient rows on the GPU.

`logits`: Unscaled log probabilities of shape [d_0, d_1, ..., $d\_(r-1)$, `num_classes`] and `dtype`, `float32`, or `float64`.

The preceding code computes sparse `softmax` cross entropy between `logits` and `labels`. The probability of a given label is considered exclusive. Soft classes are not allowed, and the label's vector must provide a single specific index for the true class for each row of `logits`.

- `tf.nn.weighted_cross_entropy_with_logits`

```
weighted_cross_entropy_with_logits(
  targets,
  logits,
  pos_weight,
  name=None
)
```

`targets`: A tensor of the same type and shape as logits.
`logits`: A tensor of type `float32` or `float64`.
`pos_weight`: A coefficient to use on the positive examples.

This is similar to `sigmoid_cross_entropy_with_logits()` except that `pos_weight` allows a trade-off of recall and precision by up or down weighting the cost of a positive error relative to a negative error.

Analyzing the Iris dataset

Let's look at a feedforward example using the Iris dataset.

 You can download the dataset from `https://github.com/ml-resources/ neuralnetwork-programming/blob/ed1/ch02/iris/iris.csv` and the target labels from `https://github.com/ml-resources/neuralnetwork- programming/blob/ed1/ch02/iris/target.csv`.

In the Iris dataset, we will use 150 rows of data made up of 50 samples from each of three Iris species: Iris setosa, Iris virginica, and Iris versicolor.

Petal geometry compared from three iris species:
Iris Setosa, **Iris Virginica**, and **Iris Versicolor**.

Iris Setosa

Iris Versicolor

Iris Virginica

In the dataset, each row contains data for each flower sample: sepal length, sepal width, petal length, petal width, and flower species. Flower species are stored as integers, with 0 denoting Iris setosa, 1 denoting Iris versicolor, and 2 denoting Iris virginica.

First, we will create a `run()` function that takes three parameters--hidden layer size `h_size`, standard deviation for weights `stddev`, and Step size of Stochastic Gradient Descent `sgd_step`:

```
def run(h_size, stddev, sgd_step)
```

Input data loading is done using the `genfromtxt` function in `numpy`. The Iris data loaded has a shape of L: 150 and W: 4. Data is loaded in the `all_X` variable. Target labels are loaded from `target.csv` in `all_Y` with the shape of L: 150, W:3:

```
def load_iris_data():
    from numpy import genfromtxt
    data = genfromtxt('iris.csv', delimiter=',')
```

```
target = genfromtxt('target.csv', delimiter=',').astype(int)
# Prepend the column of 1s for bias
L, W  = data.shape
all_X = np.ones((L, W + 1))
all_X[:, 1:] = data
num_labels = len(np.unique(target))
all_y = np.eye(num_labels)[target]
return train_test_split(all_X, all_y, test_size=0.33,
random_state=RANDOMSEED)
```

Once data is loaded, we initialize the weights matrix based on x_size, y_size, and h_size with standard deviation passed to the run() method:

- x_size= 5
- y_size= 3
- h_size= 128 (or any other number chosen for neurons in the hidden layer)

```
# Size of Layers
x_size = train_x.shape[1] # Input nodes: 4 features and 1 bias
y_size = train_y.shape[1] # Outcomes (3 iris flowers)
# variables
X = tf.placeholder("float", shape=[None, x_size])
y = tf.placeholder("float", shape=[None, y_size])
weights_1 = initialize_weights((x_size, h_size), stddev)
weights_2 = initialize_weights((h_size, y_size), stddev)
```

Next, we make the prediction using sigmoid as the activation function defined in the forward_propagration() function:

```
def forward_propagation(X, weights_1, weights_2):
    sigmoid = tf.nn.sigmoid(tf.matmul(X, weights_1))
    y = tf.matmul(sigmoid, weights_2)
    return y
```

First, sigmoid output is calculated from input X and weights_1. This is then used to calculate y as a matrix multiplication of sigmoid and weights_2:

```
y_pred = forward_propagation(X, weights_1, weights_2)
predict = tf.argmax(y_pred, dimension=1)
```

Next, we define the cost function and optimization using gradient descent. Let's look at the `GradientDescentOptimizer` being used. It is defined in the `tf.train.GradientDescentOptimizer` class and implements the gradient descent algorithm.

To construct an instance, we use the following constructor and pass `sgd_step` as a parameter:

```
# constructor for GradientDescentOptimizer
__init__(
  learning_rate,
  use_locking=False,
  name='GradientDescent'
)
```

Arguments passed are explained here:

- `learning_rate`: A tensor or a floating point value. The learning rate to use.
- `use_locking`: If True, use locks for update operations.
- `name`: Optional name prefix for the operations created when applying gradients. The default name is `"GradientDescent"`.

The following list shows the code to implement the `cost` function:

```
cost = tf.reduce_mean(tf.nn.softmax_cross_entropy_with_logits(labels=y,
logits=y_pred))
updates_sgd = tf.train.GradientDescentOptimizer(sgd_step).minimize(cost)
```

Next, we will implement the following steps:

1. Initialize the TensorFlow session:

   ```
   sess = tf.Session()
   ```

2. Initialize all the variables using `tf.initialize_all_variables()`; the return object is used to instantiate the session.
3. Iterate over `steps` (1 to 50).
4. For each step in `train_x` and `train_y`, execute `updates_sgd`.
5. Calculate the `train_accuracy` and `test_accuracy`.

We stored the accuracy for each step in a list so that we could plot a graph:

```
init = tf.initialize_all_variables()
steps = 50
sess.run(init)
x   = np.arange(steps)
test_acc = []
train_acc = []
print("Step, train accuracy, test accuracy")
for step in range(steps):
    # Train with each example
    for i in range(len(train_x)):
        sess.run(updates_sgd, feed_dict={X: train_x[i: i + 1], y:
train_y[i: i + 1]})

    train_accuracy = np.mean(np.argmax(train_y, axis=1) ==
                            sess.run(predict, feed_dict={X: train_x,
y: train_y}))
    test_accuracy = np.mean(np.argmax(test_y, axis=1) ==
                            sess.run(predict, feed_dict={X: test_x, y:
test_y}))

    print("%d, %.2f%%, %.2f%%"
          % (step + 1, 100. * train_accuracy, 100. * test_accuracy))
    test_acc.append(100. * test_accuracy)
    train_acc.append(100. * train_accuracy)
```

Code execution

Let's run this code for h_size of 128, standard deviation of 0.1, and sgd_step of 0.01:

```
def run(h_size, stddev, sgd_step):
  ...

def main():
run(128,0.1,0.01)

if __name__ == '__main__':
main()
```

The preceding code outputs the following graph, which plots the steps versus the test and train accuracy:

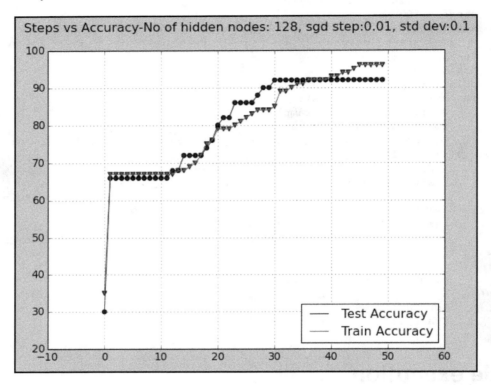

Let's compare the change in SGD steps and its effect on training accuracy. The following code is very similar to the previous code example, but we will rerun it for multiple SGD steps to see how SGD steps affect accuracy levels.

```
def run(h_size, stddev, sgd_steps):
    ....
    test_accs = []
    train_accs = []
    time_taken_summary = []
    for sgd_step in sgd_steps:
        start_time = time.time()
        updates_sgd =
tf.train.GradientDescentOptimizer(sgd_step).minimize(cost)
        sess = tf.Session()
        init = tf.initialize_all_variables()
        steps = 50
        sess.run(init)
```

```
x   = np.arange(steps)
test_acc = []
train_acc = []

print("Step, train accuracy, test accuracy")


for step in range(steps):
        # Train with each example
        for i in range(len(train_x)):
            sess.run(updates_sgd, feed_dict={X: train_x[i: i + 1],
                    y: train_y[i: i + 1]})

        train_accuracy = np.mean(np.argmax(train_y, axis=1) ==
                                    sess.run(predict,
                                    feed_dict={X: train_x, y:
train_y}))
        test_accuracy = np.mean(np.argmax(test_y, axis=1) ==
                                    sess.run(predict,
                                    feed_dict={X: test_x, y: test_y}))

        print("%d, %.2f%%, %.2f%%"
                % (step + 1, 100. * train_accuracy, 100. *
test_accuracy))
        #x.append(step)
        test_acc.append(100. * test_accuracy)
        train_acc.append(100. * train_accuracy)
    end_time = time.time()
    diff = end_time -start_time
    time_taken_summary.append((sgd_step,diff))
    t = [np.array(test_acc)]
    t.append(train_acc)
    train_accs.append(train_acc)
```

Output of the preceding code will be an array with training and test accuracy for each SGD step value. In our example, we called the function `sgd_steps` for an SGD step value of [0.01, 0.02, 0.03]:

```
def main():
    sgd_steps = [0.01,0.02,0.03]
    run(128,0.1,sgd_steps)

if __name__ == '__main__':
    main()
```

This is the plot showing how training accuracy changes with `sgd_steps`. For an SGD value of `0.03`, it reaches a higher accuracy faster as the step size is larger.

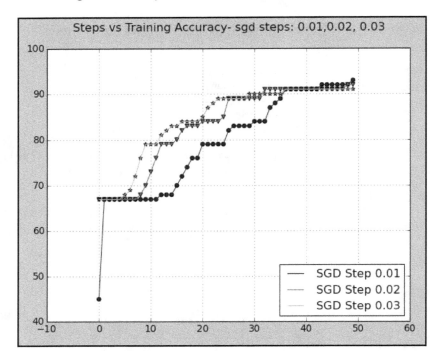

Implementing feedforward networks with images

Now we will look at how to use feedforward networks to classify images. We will be using `notMNIST` data. The dataset consists of images for nine letters, A to I.

NotMNIST dataset is similar to MNIST dataset but focuses on Alphabets instead of numbers (`http://yaroslavvb.blogspot.in/2011/09/notmnist-dataset.html`)

We have reduced the original dataset to a smaller version for the training so that you can easily get started. Download the ZIP files and extract them to the folder where the dataset is contained, `https://1drv.ms/f/s!Av6fk5nQi2j-kniw-8GtP8sdWejs`.

The pickle module of python implements an algorithm for serializing and de-serializing a Python object structure. **Pickling** is the process in which a Python object hierarchy is converted into a byte stream, unpickling is the inverse operation, where a byte stream is converted back into an object hierarchy. Pickling (and unpickling) is alternatively known as **serialization, marshaling,** [1] or **flattening**.

First, we load the images in `numpy.ndarray` from the following list of folders using the `maybe_pickle(..)` method:

```
test_folders = ['./notMNIST_small/A', './notMNIST_small/B',
'./notMNIST_small/C', './notMNIST_small/D',
'./notMNIST_small/E', './notMNIST_small/F', './notMNIST_small/G',
'./notMNIST_small/H',
'./notMNIST_small/I', './notMNIST_small/J']
train_folders = ['./notMNIST_large_v2/A', './notMNIST_large_v2/B',
'./notMNIST_large_v2/C', './notMNIST_large_v2/D',
'./notMNIST_large_v2/E', './notMNIST_large_v2/F', './notMNIST_large_v2/G',
'./notMNIST_large_v2/H',
'./notMNIST_large_v2/I', './notMNIST_large_v2/J']
maybe_pickle(data_folders, min_num_images_per_class, force=False):
```

The `maybe_pickle` uses the `load_letter` method to load the image to `ndarray` from a single folder:

```
def load_letter(folder, min_num_images):
  image_files = os.listdir(folder)
  dataset = np.ndarray(shape=(len(image_files), image_size, image_size),
                       dtype=np.float32)
  num_images = 0
  for image in image_files:
    image_file = os.path.join(folder, image)
    try:
      image_data = (ndimage.imread(image_file).astype(float) -
                    pixel_depth / 2) / pixel_depth
      if image_data.shape != (image_size, image_size):
        raise Exception('Unexpected image shape: %s' %
str(image_data.shape))
      dataset[num_images, :, :] = image_data
      num_images = num_images + 1
    except IOError as e:
      print('Could not read:', image_file, ':', e, '- it\'s ok, skipping.')
  dataset = dataset[0:num_images, :, :]
  if num_images < min_num_images:
    raise Exception('Fewer images than expected: %d < %d' %
                    (num_images, min_num_images))
  print('Dataset tensor:', dataset.shape)
```

```
print('Mean:', np.mean(dataset))
print('Standard deviation:', np.std(dataset))
return dataset
```

The `maybe_pickle` method is called for two sets of folders, `train_folders` and `test_folders`:

```
train_datasets = maybe_pickle(train_folders, 100)
test_datasets = maybe_pickle(test_folders, 50)
```

Output is similar to the following screenshot.

The first screenshot shows the `dataset_names` list variable value:

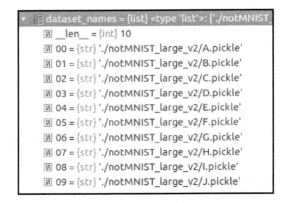

The following screenshot shows the value of the `dataset_names` variable for the `notMNIST_small` dataset:

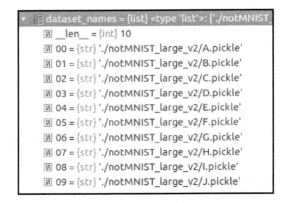

Next, `merge_datasets` is called, where pickle files from each character are combined into the following `ndarray`:

- `valid_dataset`
- `valid_labels`
- `train_dataset`
- `train_labels`

```
train_size = 1000
valid_size = 500
test_size = 500

valid_dataset, valid_labels, train_dataset, train_labels = merge_datasets(
    train_datasets, train_size, valid_size)
  _, _, test_dataset, test_labels = merge_datasets(test_datasets,
test_size)
```

Output of the preceding code is listed as follows:

```
Training dataset and labels shape: (1000, 28, 28) (1000,)
Validation dataset and labels shape: (500, 28, 28) (500,)
Testing dataset and labels shape: (500, 28, 28) (500,)
```

Finally, the `noMNIST.pickle` file is created by storing each of these `ndarray` in key-value pairs where the keys are `train_dataset`, `train_labels`, `valid_dataset`, `valid_labels`, `test_dataset`, and `test_labels`, and values are the respective `ndarray`, as shown in the following code:

```
try:
  f = open(pickle_file, 'wb')
  save = {
    'train_dataset': train_dataset,
    'train_labels': train_labels,
    'valid_dataset': valid_dataset,
    'valid_labels': valid_labels,
    'test_dataset': test_dataset,
    'test_labels': test_labels,
  }
  pickle.dump(save, f, pickle.HIGHEST_PROTOCOL)
  f.close()
except Exception as e:
  print('Unable to save data to', pickle_file, ':', e)
  raise
```

This is the full code for generating the `notMNIST.pickle` file:

```python
from __future__ import print_function
import numpy as np
import os
from scipy import ndimage
from six.moves import cPickle as pickle

data_root = '.' # Change me to store data elsewhere

num_classes = 10
np.random.seed(133)

test_folders = ['./notMNIST_small/A', './notMNIST_small/B',
'./notMNIST_small/C', './notMNIST_small/D',
                './notMNIST_small/E', './notMNIST_small/F',
'./notMNIST_small/G', './notMNIST_small/H',
                './notMNIST_small/I', './notMNIST_small/J']
train_folders = ['./notMNIST_large_v2/A', './notMNIST_large_v2/B',
'./notMNIST_large_v2/C', './notMNIST_large_v2/D',
                './notMNIST_large_v2/E', './notMNIST_large_v2/F',
'./notMNIST_large_v2/G', './notMNIST_large_v2/H',
                './notMNIST_large_v2/I', './notMNIST_large_v2/J']

image_size = 28  # Pixel width and height.
pixel_depth = 255.0

def load_letter(folder, min_num_images):
  image_files = os.listdir(folder)
  dataset = np.ndarray(shape=(len(image_files), image_size, image_size),
                       dtype=np.float32)
  num_images = 0
  for image in image_files:
    image_file = os.path.join(folder, image)
    try:
      image_data = (ndimage.imread(image_file).astype(float) -
                  pixel_depth / 2) / pixel_depth
      if image_data.shape != (image_size, image_size):
        raise Exception('Unexpected image shape: %s' %
str(image_data.shape))
      dataset[num_images, :, :] = image_data
      num_images = num_images + 1
    except IOError as e:
      print('Could not read:', image_file, ':', e, '- it\'s ok, skipping.')
  dataset = dataset[0:num_images, :, :]
  if num_images < min_num_images:
    raise Exception('Fewer images than expected: %d < %d' %
                    (num_images, min_num_images))
```

```
    print('Dataset tensor:', dataset.shape)
    print('Mean:', np.mean(dataset))
    print('Standard deviation:', np.std(dataset))
    return dataset
def maybe_pickle(data_folders, min_num_images_per_class, force=False):
    dataset_names = []
    for folder in data_folders:
        set_filename = folder + '.pickle'
        dataset_names.append(set_filename)
        if os.path.exists(set_filename) and not force:
            print('%s already present - Skipping pickling.' % set_filename)
        else:
            print('Pickling %s.' % set_filename)
            dataset = load_letter(folder, min_num_images_per_class)
            try:
                with open(set_filename, 'wb') as f:
                    #pickle.dump(dataset, f, pickle.HIGHEST_PROTOCOL)
                    print(pickle.HIGHEST_PROTOCOL)
                    pickle.dump(dataset, f, 2)
            except Exception as e:
                print('Unable to save data to', set_filename, ':', e)
    return dataset_names

def make_arrays(nb_rows, img_size):
    if nb_rows:
        dataset = np.ndarray((nb_rows, img_size, img_size), dtype=np.float32)
        labels = np.ndarray(nb_rows, dtype=np.int32)
    else:
        dataset, labels = None, None
```

Let's look at how the pickle file created earlier loads data and runs a network with one hidden layer.

First, we will load the training, testing, and validation datasets (ndarray) from the notMNIST.pickle file:

```
with open(pickle_file, 'rb') as f:
 save = pickle.load(f)
 training_dataset = save['train_dataset']
 training_labels = save['train_labels']
 validation_dataset = save['valid_dataset']
 validation_labels = save['valid_labels']
 test_dataset = save['test_dataset']
 test_labels = save['test_labels']

print 'Training set', training_dataset.shape, training_labels.shape
print 'Validation set', validation_dataset.shape, validation_labels.shape
print 'Test set', test_dataset.shape, test_labels.shape
```

You will see an output similar to the following listing:

```
Training set (1000, 28, 28) (1000,)
Validation set (500, 28, 28) (500,)
Test set (500, 28, 28) (500,)
```

Next, we `reformat` the `dataset` into a two-dimensional array so that data is easier to process with TensorFlow:

```
def reformat(dataset, labels):
  dataset = dataset.reshape((-1, image_size *
image_size)).astype(np.float32)
  # Map 0 to [1.0, 0.0, 0.0 ...], 1 to [0.0, 1.0, 0.0 ...]
  labels = (np.arange(num_of_labels) == labels[:, None]).astype(np.float32)
  return dataset, labels
train_dataset, train_labels = reformat(training_dataset, training_labels)
  valid_dataset, valid_labels = reformat(validation_dataset,
validation_labels)
  test_dataset, test_labels = reformat(test_dataset, test_labels)

  print 'Training dataset shape', train_dataset.shape, train_labels.shape
  print 'Validation dataset shape', valid_dataset.shape, valid_labels.shape
  print 'Test dataset shape', test_dataset.shape, test_labels.shape
```

You will see the following output:

```
Training dataset shape (1000, 784) (1000, 10)
Validation dataset shape (500, 784) (500, 10)
Test dataset shape (500, 784) (500, 10)
```

Next, we define the graph that will return the content to which all the variables will be loaded.

The size of each weight and bias is listed here, where `image_size` = 28 and `no_of_neurons` = 1024.

 Number of neurons in the hidden layer should be optimal. Too few neurons leads to lower accuracy, while too high a number leads to overfitting.

Layer in the neural network	Weight	Bias
1	row = 28 x 28 = 784 columns = 1024	1024
2	row = 1024 columns = 10	10

We will initialize the TensorFlow graph and initialize placeholder variables from training, validation, and test the datasets and labels.

We will also define weights and biases for two layers:

```
graph = tf.Graph()
 no_of_neurons = 1024
 with graph.as_default():
    # Placeholder that will be fed
    # at run time with a training minibatch in the session
    tf_train_dataset = tf.placeholder(tf.float32,
      shape=(batch_size, image_size * image_size))
    tf_train_labels = tf.placeholder(tf.float32, shape=(batch_size,
num_of_labels))
    tf_valid_dataset = tf.constant(valid_dataset)
    tf_test_dataset = tf.constant(test_dataset)

    # Variables.
    w1 = tf.Variable(tf.truncated_normal([image_size * image_size,
no_of_neurons]))
    b1 = tf.Variable(tf.zeros([no_of_neurons]))

    w2 = tf.Variable(
    tf.truncated_normal([no_of_neurons, num_of_labels]))
    b2 = tf.Variable(tf.zeros([num_of_labels]))
```

Next, we define the hidden layer tensor and the calculated logit:

```
hidden1 = tf.nn.relu(tf.matmul(tf_train_dataset, w1) + b1)
logits = tf.matmul(hidden1, w2) + b2
```

Loss function for our network is going to be based on the `softmax` function applied over cross entropy with `logits`:

```
loss = tf.reduce_mean(
     tf.nn.softmax_cross_entropy_with_logits(logits=logits,
labels=tf_train_labels))
# Training computation.

loss = tf.reduce_mean(
     tf.nn.softmax_cross_entropy_with_logits(logits=logits,
labels=tf_train_labels))

    # Optimizer.
    optimizer = tf.train.GradientDescentOptimizer(0.5).minimize(loss)
```

Next, we calculate the `logits` (predicted values); note that we are using `softmax` to normalize the `logits`:

```
train_prediction = tf.nn.softmax(logits)
```

Calculate the test and validation predictions. Notice the activation function `RELU` being used here to calculate `w1` and `b1`:

```
tf.nn.relu(tf.matmul(tf_valid_dataset, w1) + b1)
  valid_prediction = tf.nn.softmax(
      tf.matmul( tf.nn.relu(tf.matmul(tf_valid_dataset, w1) + b1),
                 w2
               ) + b2)
  test_prediction = tf.nn.softmax(
      tf.matmul(tf.nn.relu(tf.matmul(tf_test_dataset, w1) + b1), w2) + b2)
```

Now we will create a TensorFlow session and pass the datasets loaded through the neural network created:

```
with tf.Session(graph=graph) as session:
  tf.initialize_all_variables().run()
  print("Initialized")
  for step in xrange(num_steps):
    offset = (step * batch_size) % (train_labels.shape[0] - batch_size)
    # Generate a minibatch.
    batch_data = train_dataset[offset:(offset + batch_size), :]
    batch_labels = train_labels[offset:(offset + batch_size), :]
    feed_dict = {tf_train_dataset: batch_data, tf_train_labels:
batch_labels}
    _, l, predictions = session.run(
      [optimizer, loss, train_prediction], feed_dict=feed_dict)
    minibatch_accuracy = accuracy(predictions, batch_labels)
    validation_accuracy = accuracy(
     valid_prediction.eval(), valid_labels)
    if (step % 10 == 0):
      print("Minibatch loss at step", step, ":", l)
      print("Minibatch accuracy: %.1f%%" % accuracy(predictions,
batch_labels))
      print("Validation accuracy: %.1f%%" % validation_accuracy)
minibatch_acc.append( minibatch_accuracy)
validation_acc.append( validation_accuracy)
t = [np.array(minibatch_acc)]
t.append(validation_acc)
```

The full code can be found at `https://github.com/rajdeepd/`
`neuralnetwork-programming/blob/ed1/ch02/nomnist/singlelayer-`
`neural_network.py`.

The complete code can be found at the preceding GitHub link. Notice that we are
appending the validation and minibatch accuracy to an array that we will plot:

```
print("Test accuracy: %.1f%%" % accuracy(test_prediction.eval(),
test_labels))
title = "NotMNIST DataSet - Single Hidden Layer - 1024 neurons Activation
function: RELU"
label = ['Minibatch Accuracy', 'Validation Accuracy']
draw_plot(x, t, title, label)
```

Let's look at the plot generated by the preceding code:

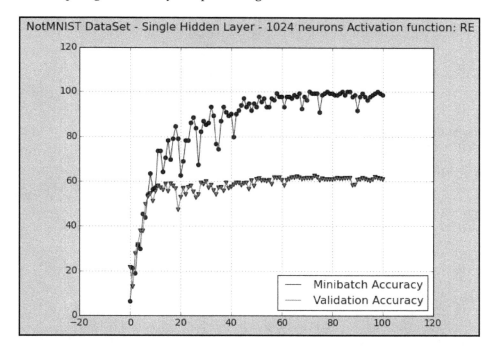

Minibatch accuracy reaches 100 by iteration number 8- while validation accuracy stops at
60.

Analyzing the effect of activation functions on the feedforward networks accuracy

In the previous example, we used RELU as the activation function. TensorFlow supports multiple activation functions. Let's look at how each of these activation functions affects validation accuracy. We will generate some random values:

```
x_val = np.linspace(start=-10., stop=10., num=1000)
```

Then generate the activation output:

```
# ReLU activation
 y_relu = session.run(tf.nn.relu(x_val))
 # ReLU-6 activation
 y_relu6 = session.run(tf.nn.relu6(x_val))
 # Sigmoid activation
 y_sigmoid = session.run(tf.nn.sigmoid(x_val))
 # Hyper Tangent activation
 y_tanh = session.run(tf.nn.tanh(x_val))
 # Softsign activation
 y_softsign = session.run(tf.nn.softsign(x_val))

 # Softplus activation
 y_softplus = session.run(tf.nn.softplus(x_val))
 # Exponential linear activation
 y_elu = session.run(tf.nn.elu(x_val))
```

Plot the activation against x_val:

```
plt.plot(x_val, y_softplus, 'r--', label='Softplus', linewidth=2)
plt.plot(x_val, y_relu, 'b:', label='RELU', linewidth=2)
plt.plot(x_val, y_relu6, 'g-.', label='RELU6', linewidth=2)
plt.plot(x_val, y_elu, 'k-', label='ELU', linewidth=1)
plt.ylim([-1.5,7])
plt.legend(loc='top left')
plt.title('Activation functions', y=1.05)
plt.show()
plt.plot(x_val, y_sigmoid, 'r--', label='Sigmoid', linewidth=2)
plt.plot(x_val, y_tanh, 'b:', label='tanh', linewidth=2)
plt.plot(x_val, y_softsign, 'g-.', label='Softsign', linewidth=2)
plt.ylim([-1.5,1.5])
plt.legend(loc='top left')
plt.title('Activation functions with Vanishing Gradient', y=1.05)
plt.show()
```

Plots are shown in the following screenshot:

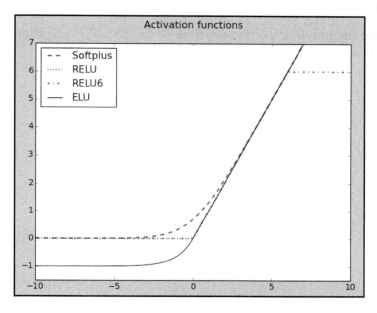

The plot comparing **Activation functions with Vanishing Gradient** is as follows:

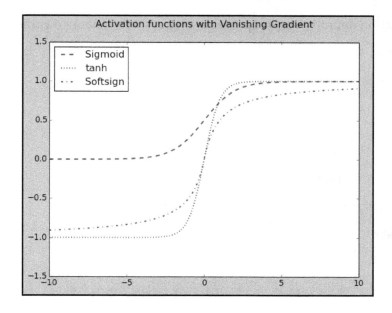

Now let's look at the activation function and how it affects validation accuracy for NotMNIST data.

We have modified the previous example so that we can pass the activation function as a parameter in `main()`:

```
RELU = 'RELU'
RELU6 = 'RELU6'
CRELU = 'CRELU'
SIGMOID = 'SIGMOID'
ELU = 'ELU'
SOFTPLUS = 'SOFTPLUS'
def activation(name, features):
  if name == RELU:
    return tf.nn.relu(features)
  if name == RELU6:
    return tf.nn.relu6(features)
  if name == SIGMOID:
    return tf.nn.sigmoid(features)
  if name == CRELU:
    return tf.nn.crelu(features)
  if name == ELU:
    return tf.nn.elu(features)
  if name == SOFTPLUS:
    return tf.nn.softplus(features)
```

The `run()` function definition encompasses the login that we defined earlier:

```
batch_size = 128
#activations = [RELU, RELU6, SIGMOID, CRELU, ELU, SOFTPLUS]
activations = [RELU, RELU6, SIGMOID, ELU, SOFTPLUS]
plot_loss = False
def run(name):
 print(name)
 with open(pickle_file, 'rb') as f:
   save = pickle.load(f)
   training_dataset = save['train_dataset']
   training_labels = save['train_labels']
   validation_dataset = save['valid_dataset']
   validation_labels = save['valid_labels']
   test_dataset = save['test_dataset']
   test_labels = save['test_labels']
 train_dataset, train_labels = reformat(training_dataset, training_labels)
 valid_dataset, valid_labels = reformat(validation_dataset,
   validation_labels)
 test_dataset, test_labels = reformat(test_dataset, test_labels)
 graph = tf.Graph()
 no_of_neurons = 1024
```

```
with graph.as_default():

tf_train_dataset = tf.placeholder(tf.float32,
shape=(batch_size, image_size * image_size))
tf_train_labels = tf.placeholder(tf.float32, shape=(batch_size,
  num_of_labels))
tf_valid_dataset = tf.constant(valid_dataset)
tf_test_dataset = tf.constant(test_dataset)
# Define Variables.
# Training computation...
# Optimizer ..
# Predictions for the training, validation, and test data.
train_prediction = tf.nn.softmax(logits)
valid_prediction = tf.nn.softmax(
tf.matmul(activation(name,tf.matmul(tf_valid_dataset, w1) + b1), w2) + b2)
test_prediction = tf.nn.softmax(
tf.matmul(activation(name,tf.matmul(tf_test_dataset, w1) + b1), w2) + b2)

num_steps = 101
minibatch_acc = []
validation_acc = []
loss_array = []
with tf.Session(graph=graph) as session:
  tf.initialize_all_variables().run()
  print("Initialized")
  for step in xrange(num_steps):
    offset = (step * batch_size) % (train_labels.shape[0] - batch_size)
    # Generate a minibatch.
    batch_data = train_dataset[offset:(offset + batch_size), :]
    batch_labels = train_labels[offset:(offset + batch_size), :]
    feed_dict = {tf_train_dataset: batch_data, tf_train_labels:
batch_labels}

    _, l, predictions = session.run(
      [optimizer, loss, train_prediction], feed_dict=feed_dict)
    minibatch_accuracy = accuracy(predictions, batch_labels)
    validation_accuracy = accuracy(
     valid_prediction.eval(), valid_labels)
    if (step % 10 == 0):
      print("Minibatch loss at step", step, ":", l)
      print("Minibatch accuracy: %.1f%%" % accuracy(predictions,
        batch_labels))
      print("Validation accuracy: %.1f%%" % accuracy(
    valid_prediction.eval(), valid_labels))
    minibatch_acc.append(minibatch_accuracy)
    validation_acc.append(validation_accuracy)
    loss_array.append(l)
    print("Test accuracy: %.1f%%" % accuracy(test_prediction.eval(),
```

```
       test_labels))
    return validation_acc, loss_array
```

Plots from the preceding list are shown in the following screenshot:

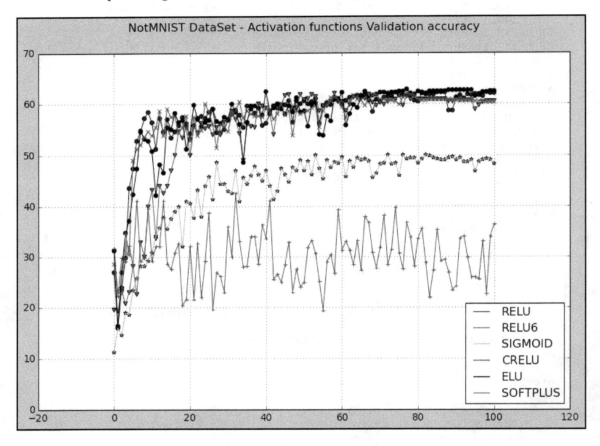

Validation accuracy for various activation functions

As can be seen in the preceding graphs, **RELU** and **RELU6** provide maximum validation accuracy, which is close to 60 percent. Now let's look at how training loss behaves as we progress through the steps for various activations:

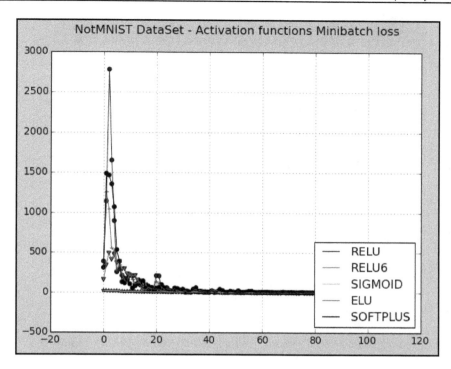

Training loss for various activations as a function of steps

Training loss converges to zero for most of the activation functions, though **RELU** is the least effective in the short-term.

Summary

In this chapter, we built our first neural network, which was feedforward only, and used it for classification with the Iris dataset and later the NotMNIST dataset. You learned how various activation functions like affect the validation accuracy of the prediction.

In the next chapter, we will explore a convoluted neural network, which is more advanced and effective for an image dataset.

3
Optimization for Neural Networks

A number of applications in deep learning require optimization problems to be solved. Optimization refers to bringing whatever we are dealing with towards its ultimate state. The problem solved through the use of an optimization process must be supplied with data, providing model constants and parameters in functions, describing the overall objective function along with some constraints.

In this chapter, we will look at the TensorFlow pipeline and various optimization models provided by the TensorFlow library. The list of topics covered are as follows:

- Optimization basics
- Types of optimizers
- Gradient descent
- Choosing the correct optimizer

What is optimization?

The process to find maxima or minima is based on constraints. The choice of optimization algorithm for your deep learning model can mean the difference between good results in minutes, hours, and days.

Optimization sits at the center of deep learning. Most learning problems reduce to optimization problems. Let's imagine we are solving a problem for some set of data. Using this pre-processed data, we train a model by solving an optimization problem, which optimizes the weights of the model with regards to the chosen loss function and some regularization function.

Hyper parameters of a model play a significant role in the efficient training of a model. Therefore, it is essential to use the different optimization strategies and algorithms to measure appropriate and optimum values of model's hyper parameters, which affect our Model's learning process, and finally the output of a model.

Types of optimizers

First, we look at the high-level categories of optimization algorithms and then dive deep into the individual optimizers.

First order optimization algorithms minimize or maximize a loss function using its gradient values concerning the parameters. The popularly used First order optimization algorithm is gradient descent. Here, the first order derivative tells us whether the function is decreasing or increasing at a particular point. The first order derivative gives us a line which is tangential to a point on its error surface.

The derivative for a function depends on single variables, whereas a gradient for a function depends on multiple variables.

Second order optimization algorithms use the second order derivative, which is also known as **Hessian**, to minimize or maximize the given loss function. Here, the Hessian is a matrix of second order partial derivatives. The second derivative is costly to compute. Hence, it's not used much. The second order derivative indicates to us whether the first derivative is increasing or decreasing, giving an idea of functions curvature. The second order derivative gives us with a quadratic surface which touches the shape of the error surface.

The second order derivative is costly to compute, but the advantage of a second order optimization method is that it does not neglect or ignore the curvature of a surface. Also, the stepwise performance is better. The key thing to note while choosing the optimization method is, first-order optimization methods are simple to compute and less time consuming, converging rather fast on large data sets. Second order methods are faster only when the second order derivative is known, and these methods are slower and expensive to compute in terms of both time and memory.

The second order optimization method can, at times, work better than first-order gradient descent methods because second-order methods will never get stuck around paths of slow convergence, that is, around saddle points, whereas gradient descent at times gets stuck and does not converge.

Gradient descent

Gradient descent is an algorithm which minimizes functions. A set of parameters defines a function, and the gradient descent algorithm starts with the initial set of param values and iteratively moves toward a set of param values that minimizes the function.

This iterative minimization is achieved using calculus, taking steps in the negative direction of the function gradient, as can be seen in the following diagram:

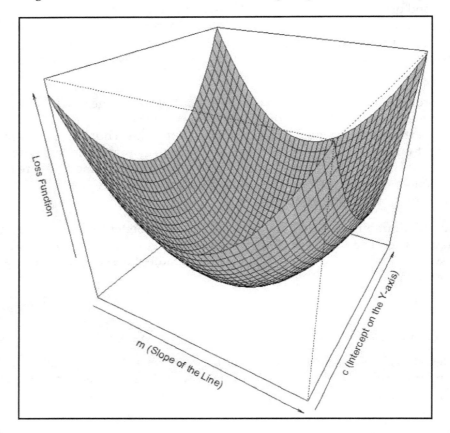

Gradient descent is the most successful optimization algorithm. As mentioned earlier, it is used to do weights updates in a neural network so that we minimize the loss function. Let's now talk about an important neural network method called backpropagation, in which we firstly propagate forward and calculate the dot product of inputs with their corresponding weights, and then apply an activation function to the sum of products which transforms the input to an output and adds non linearities to the model, which enables the model to learn almost any arbitrary functional mappings.

Later, we back propagate in the neural network, carrying error terms and updating weights values using gradient descent, as shown in the following graph:

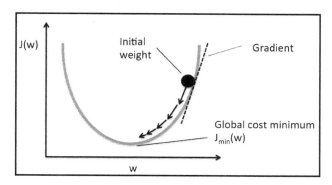

Different variants of gradient descent

Standard gradient descent, also known as **batch gradient descent**, will calculate the gradient of the whole dataset but will perform only one update. Therefore, it can be quite slow and tough to control for datasets which are extremely large and don't fit in the memory. Let's now look at algorithms that can solve this problem.

Stochastic gradient descent (**SGD**) performs parameter updates on each training example, whereas mini batch performs an update with *n* number of training examples in each batch. The issue with SGD is that, due to the frequent updates and fluctuations, it eventually complicates the convergence to the accurate minimum and will keep exceeding due to regular fluctuations. Mini-batch gradient descent comes to the rescue here, which reduces the variance in the parameter update, leading to a much better and stable convergence. SGD and mini-batch are used interchangeably.

Overall problems with gradient descent include choosing a proper learning rate so that we avoid slow convergence at small values, or divergence at larger values and applying the same learning rate to all parameter updates wherein if the data is sparse we might not want to update all of them to the same extent. Lastly, is dealing with saddle points.

Algorithms to optimize gradient descent

We will now be looking at various methods for optimizing gradient descent in order to calculate different learning rates for each parameter, calculate momentum, and prevent decaying learning rates.

To solve the problem of high variance oscillation of the SGD, a method called **momentum** was discovered; this accelerates the SGD by navigating along the appropriate direction and softening the oscillations in irrelevant directions. Basically, it adds a fraction of the update vector of the past step to the current update vector. Momentum value is usually set to .9. Momentum leads to a faster and stable convergence with reduced oscillations.

Nesterov accelerated gradient explains that as we reach the minima, that is, the lowest point on the curve, momentum is quite high and it doesn't know to slow down at that point due to the large momentum which could cause it to miss the minima entirely and continue moving up. Nesterov proposed that we first make a long jump based on the previous momentum, then calculate the gradient and then make a correction which results in a parameter update. Now, this update prevents us to go too fast and not miss the minima, and makes it more responsive to changes.

Adagrad allows the learning rate to adapt based on the parameters. Therefore, it performs large updates for infrequent parameters and small updates for frequent parameters. Therefore, it is very well-suited for dealing with sparse data. The main flaw is that its learning rate is always decreasing and decaying. Problems with decaying learning rates are solved using AdaDelta.

AdaDelta solves the problem of decreasing learning rate in AdaGrad. In AdaGrad, the learning rate is computed as one divided by the sum of square roots. At each stage, we add another square root to the sum, which causes the denominator to decrease constantly. Now, instead of summing all prior square roots, it uses a sliding window which allows the sum to decrease.

Adaptive Moment Estimation (**Adam**) computes adaptive learning rates for each parameter. Like AdaDelta, Adam not only stores the decaying average of past squared gradients but additionally stores the momentum change for each parameter. Adam works well in practice and is one of the most used optimization methods today.

The following two images (image credit: Alec Radford) show the optimization behavior of optimization algorithms described earlier. We see their behavior on the contours of a loss surface over time. Adagrad, RMsprop, and Adadelta almost quickly head off in the right direction and converge fast, whereas momentum and NAG are headed off-track. NAG is soon able to correct its course due to its improved responsiveness by looking ahead and going to the minimum.

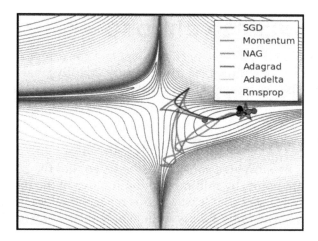

The second image displays the behavior of the algorithms at a saddle point. **SGD**, **Momentum**, and **NAG** find it challenging to break symmetry, but slowly they manage to escape the saddle point, whereas **Adagrad**, **Adadelta**, and **RMsprop** head down the negative slope, as can be seen from the following image:

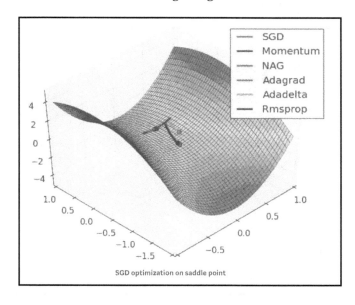

Which optimizer to choose

In the case that the input data is sparse or if we want fast convergence while training complex neural networks, we get the best results using adaptive learning rate methods. We also don't need to tune the learning rate. For most cases, Adam is usually a good choice.

Optimization with an example

Let's take an example of linear regression, where we try to find the best fit for a straight line through a number of data points by minimizing the squares of the distance from the line to each data point. This is why we call it least squares regression. Essentially, we are formulating the problem as an optimization problem, where we are trying to minimize a loss function.

Let's set up input data and look at the scatter plot:

```
# input data
xData = np.arange(100, step=.1)
yData = xData + 20 * np.sin(xData/10)
```

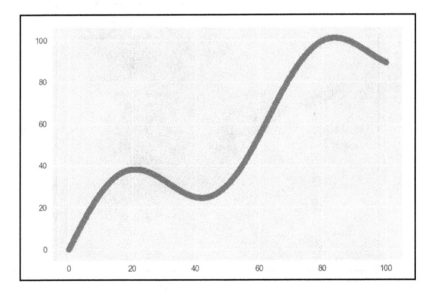

Define the data size and batch size:

```
# define the data size and batch size
nSamples = 1000
batchSize = 100
```

We will need to resize the data to meet the TensorFlow input format, as follows:

```
# resize input for tensorflow
 xData = np.reshape(xData, (nSamples, 1))
 yData = np.reshape(yData, (nSamples, 1))
```

The following scope initializes the `weights` and `bias`, and describes the linear model and loss function:

```
with tf.variable_scope("linear-regression-pipeline"):
    W = tf.get_variable("weights", (1,1),
initializer=tf.random_normal_initializer())
    b = tf.get_variable("bias", (1, ),
initializer=tf.constant_initializer(0.0))

    # model
    yPred = tf.matmul(X, W) + b
    # loss function
    loss = tf.reduce_sum((y - yPred)**2/nSamples)
```

We then set optimizers for minimizing the loss:

```
# set the optimizer
 #optimizer =
tf.train.GradientDescentOptimizer(learning_rate=0.001).minimize(loss)
 #optimizer = tf.train.AdamOptimizer(learning_rate=.001).minimize(loss)
 #optimizer = tf.train.AdadeltaOptimizer(learning_rate=.001).minimize(loss)
 #optimizer = tf.train.AdagradOptimizer(learning_rate=.001).minimize(loss)
 #optimizer = tf.train.MomentumOptimizer(learning_rate=.001,
momentum=0.9).minimize(loss)
 #optimizer = tf.train.FtrlOptimizer(learning_rate=.001).minimize(loss)
 optimizer = tf.train.RMSPropOptimizer(learning_rate=.001).minimize(loss)
We then select the mini batch and run the optimizers errors = []
 with tf.Session() as sess:
     # init variables
     sess.run(tf.global_variables_initializer())

     for _ in range(1000):
         # select mini batch
         indices = np.random.choice(nSamples, batchSize)
         xBatch, yBatch = xData[indices], yData[indices]
         # run optimizer
```

```
        _, lossVal = sess.run([optimizer, loss], feed_dict={X: xBatch, y:
yBatch})
        errors.append(lossVal)

plt.plot([np.mean(errors[i-50:i]) for i in range(len(errors))])
plt.show()
plt.savefig("errors.png")
```

The output of the preceding code is as follows:

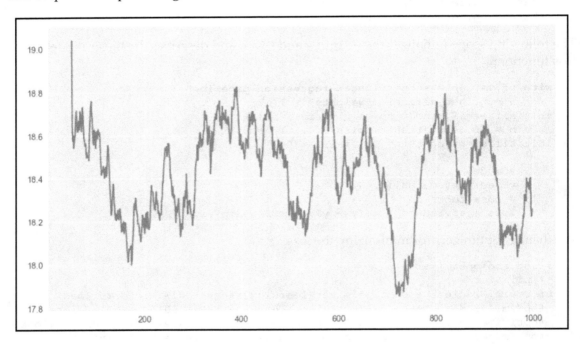

We also get a sliding curve, as follows:

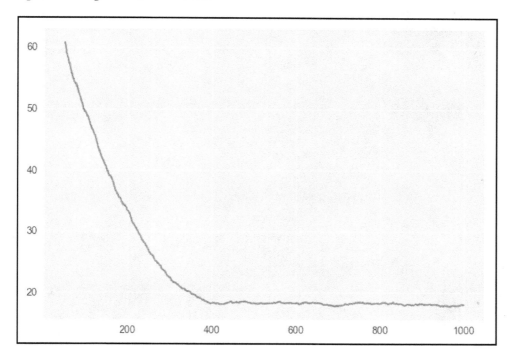

Summary

In this chapter, we learned the fundamentals of optimization techniques and various types. Optimization is a complicated subject and a lot depends on the nature and size of our data. Also, optimization depends on weight matrices. A lot of these optimizers are trained and tuned for tasks like image classification or predictions. However, for custom or new use cases, we need to perform trial and error to determine the best solution.

4
Convolutional Neural Networks

Convolutional networks (reference *LeCun[1]*, 2013), also known as **Convolutional neural networks**
or **CNNs**, are a particular type of neural network that process data with a grid-like topology. Examples include time-series data, which can be thought of as a 1D grid taking samples at regular time intervals, or image data that is a 2D grid of pixels. The name convolutional neural network means that the network employs a mathematical operation called **convolution**. Convolution is a specific kind of linear operation. Convolutional networks are neural networks that use convolution (a mathematical operation) in place of general matrix multiplication in at least one of their layers.

First, we will describe the mathematical operation of convolution. Then we will discuss the concept of pooling and how it helps CNN. We will also look at convolution networks implementation in TensorFlow.

Toward the end of this chapter, we will use TensorFlow's CNN implementation to classify dogs and cats from the Stanford dataset.

Lecun[1] : `http://yann.lecun.com/exdb/lenet/`

We will be covering the following topics in this chapter:

- An overview and the intuition of CNN
- Convolution operations
- Pooling
- Image classification with convolutional networks

An overview and the intuition of CNN

CNN consists of multiple layers of convolutions, polling and finally fully connected layers. This is much more efficient than pure feedforward networks we discussed in Chapter 2, *Deep Feedforward Networks*.

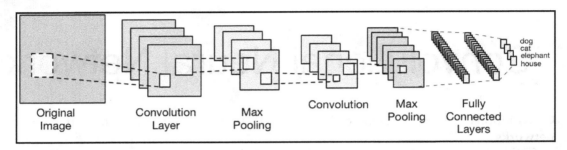

The preceding diagram takes images through **Convolution Layer** | **Max Pooling** | **Convolution** | **Max Pooling** | **Fully Connected Layers** this is an CNN architecture

Single Conv Layer Computation

Let's first discuss what the conv layer computes intuitively. The Conv layer's parameters consist of a set of learnable filters (also called **tensors**). Each filter is small spatially (depth, width, and height), but extends through the full depth of the input volume (image). A filter on the first layer of a ConvNet typically has a size of 5 x 5 x 3 (that is, five pixels width and height, and three for depth, because images have three depths for color channels). During the forward pass, filters slide (or **convolve**) across the width and height of the input volume and compute the dot product between the entries of the filter and the input at any point. As the filter slides over the width and height of the input volume, it produces a 2D activation that gives the responses of that filter at every spatial position. The network will learn filters that activate when they see some kind of visual feature, such as an edge of some orientation or a blotch of some color on the first layer, or it might detect an entire honeycomb or wheel-like patterns on higher layers of the network. Once we have an entire set of filters in each conv layer (for example, 12 filters), each of them produces a separate 2D activation map. We stack these activation maps along the depth dimension and produce the output volume.

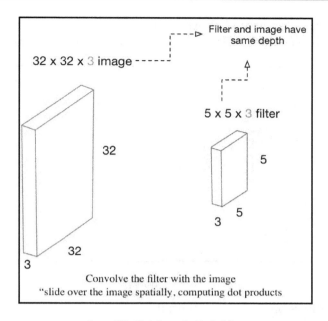

Image of 32 x 32 pixels convolved by 5 x 5 filter

The preceding image shows a 32 x 32 x 3 image on which a filter of 5 x 5 x 3 is applied.

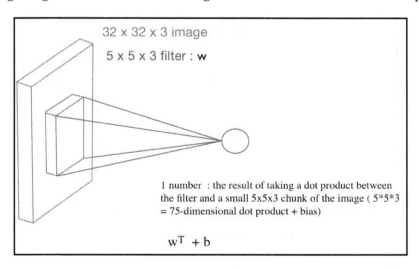

Each dot product between filter and image chunk results in a single number

Next, let's convolve the filter created above the whole image, moving it one pixel at a time. The final output will be sized 28 x 28 x 1. This is called an **activation map**.

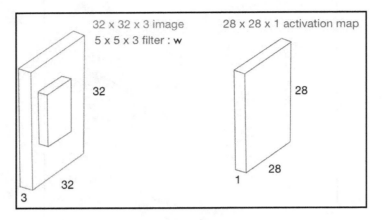

Activation map generated by applying a filter on a image

Consider using two filters one after the other; this will result in two activation maps of size 28 x 28 x 1.

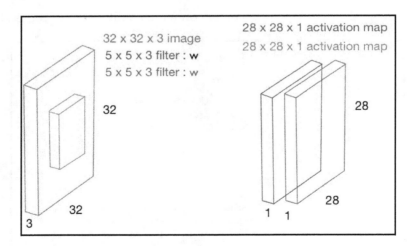

Applying two filters on a single image results in two activation maps

If we use six such filters, we will end up with a new image sized 28 x 28 x 3. A ConvNet is a sequence of such convolution layers interspersed with activation functions such as **Relu**.

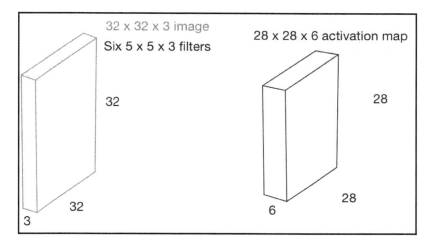

Result of applying six filters of 5 x 5 x 3 on image results in activation map of 28 x 28 x 6

Let us formally defined CNN according to TensorFlow parlance.

Definition: A CNN is a neural network that has at least one layer (tf.nn.conv2d) that makes a convolution between its input and a configurable kernel generating the layer's output. A convolution applies a kernel (filter) to every point in the input layer (a tensor). It generates a filtered output by sliding the kernel over an input tensor.

Use Case: Following example is an edge detection filter applied on an input image using a Convolution

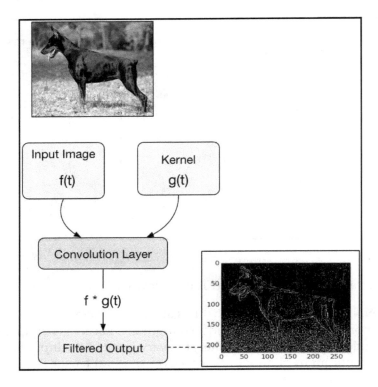

Edge detection by applying kernel on an input image

CNNs follow a process that matches information similar to the structure found in the cellular layout of a cat's striate cortex. As signals are passed through a cat's striate cortex, certain layers signal when a visual pattern is highlighted. For example, one layer of cells activates (increases its output signal) when a horizontal line passes through it. A CNN will exhibit a similar behavior where clusters of neurons activate based on patterns learned from training. After training based on prelabeled data, a CNN will have certain layers that activate when a horizontal/vertical line passes through it.

Matching horizontal/vertical lines would be a useful neural network architecture, but CNNs layer multiple simple patterns to match complex patterns. These patterns are called **filters** or **kernels**. The goal of training is to adjust these kernel weights to minimize the loss function. Training these filters is accomplished by combining multiple layers and learning weights using gradient descent or other optimization techniques.

CNN in TensorFlow

A CNN is composed of convolution layers (defined by `tf.nn.conv2d`), a non-linearity layer (`tf.nn.relu`), a max pool (`tf.nn.max_pool`), and fully connected layers (`tf.matmul`). The following image shows typical CNN layers and their corresponding implementations in TensorFlow:

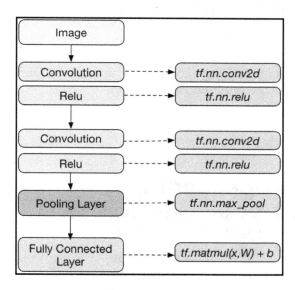

Mapping CNN layers to TensorFlow functions

Image loading in TensorFlow

Now let's look at how TensorFlow loads images. Let's define a constant with a small array of three images and load them into a session:

```
sess = tf.InteractiveSession()
image_batch = tf.constant([
    [ # First Image
        [[255, 0, 0], [255, 0, 0], [0, 255, 0]],
        [[255, 0, 0], [255, 0, 0], [0, 255, 0]]
    ],
    [ # Second Image
        [[0, 0, 0], [0, 255, 0], [0, 255, 0]],
        [[0, 0, 0], [0, 255, 0], [0, 255, 0]]
    ],
    [ # Third Image
        [[0, 0, 255], [0, 0, 255], [0, 0, 255]],
```

```
        [[0, 0, 255], [0, 0, 255], [0, 0, 255]]
    ]
])
print(image_batch.get_shape())
print(sess.run(image_batch)[1][0][0])
```

The output of the preceding listing shows the shape of the tensor and the first pixel of the first image. In this example code, an array of images is created that includes three images. Each image has a height of two pixels and a width of three pixels with an RGB color space. The output from the example code shows the number of images as the size of the first set of dimensions, Dimension(1). The height of each image is the size of the second set, Dimension(2), the width of each image comprises the third set, Dimension(3), and the array size of the color channel is the final set, Dimension(3):

```
(3, 2, 3, 3)
[255 0 0]
```

Convolution operations

Convolution operations are key components of a CNN; these operations use an input tensor and a filter to compute the output. The key is deciding the parameters available to tune them.

Suppose we are tracking the location of an object. Its output is a single *x(t)*, which is the position of the object at time *t*. Both *x* and *t* are real-valued, that is, we can get a different reading at any instant in time. Suppose that our measurement is noisy. To obtain a less noisy estimate of the object's position, we would like to average together measurements. More recent measurements are more relevant for us; we want this to be a weighted average giving higher weight to recent measurements. We can compute this using a weighting function *w(a)*, where *a* is the age of a measurement (when the measurement was taken) If we apply a weighted average operation at every moment, we obtain a new function providing a smoothed estimate of the position of the object:

$$s(t) = \int x(a)w(t-a)$$

This operation is called **convolution**. A convolution operation is denoted with an asterisk:

$$s(t) = (x * w)(t)$$

Here,

- w is the kernel
- x is the input
- s is the output, also called a **feature map**

Convolution on an image

If we use a 2D image I as our input, we probably also want to use a 2D kernel K. The preceding equation will look as follows:

$$s(i,j)=(I*K)(i,j)=\sum_m\sum_n I(m,n)*K(i-m,j-n)$$

As the convolution function is commutative, we can write the preceding equation as follows:

$$s(i,j)=(I*K)(i,j)=\sum\sum I(i-m,j-n)*K(m,n)$$

Changing i - m and j -n to additions is referred to as cross-correlation, as that is what is implemented by TensorFlow:

$$s(i,j)=(I*K)(i,j)=\sum_m\sum_n I(i+m,j+n)*K(m,n)$$

Let's define a simple input and a kernel and run the `conv2d` operation in TensorFlow. Let's take a look at a simple image input and a kernel input. The following diagram shows a basic image, a kernel, and the expected output by applying the convolution operation:

$$input = \begin{bmatrix} 1 & 1 & 1 & 0 & 0 \\ 0 & 0 & 1 & 1 & 1 \\ 0 & 0 & 1 & 1 & 0 \\ 0 & 0 & 1 & 0 & 0 \end{bmatrix} \quad kernel = \begin{bmatrix} 1 & 0 & 1 \\ 0 & 1 & 0 \\ 1 & 0 & 1 \end{bmatrix}$$

$$output = \begin{matrix} 3 & 3 & 3 \\ 2 & 2 & 4 \end{matrix}$$

Example of basic image and kernel applied to it

Now let's look at how the output is achieved with a stride of 1, 1, 1, 1:

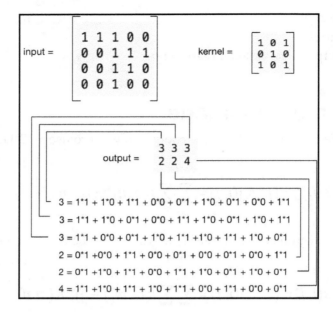

Calculating output by applying kernel to the input

Next, we will implement the same in TensorFlow:

```
i = tf.constant([
                [1.0, 1.0, 1.0, 0.0, 0.0],
                [0.0, 0.0, 1.0, 1.0, 1.0],
                [0.0, 0.0, 1.0, 1.0, 0.0],
                [0.0, 0.0, 1.0, 0.0, 0.0]], dtype=tf.float32)
k = tf.constant([
                [1.0, 0.0, 1.0],
                [0.0, 1.0, 0.0],
                [1.0, 0.0, 1.0]
         ], dtype=tf.float32),
kernel = tf.reshape(k, [3, 3, 1, 1], name='kernel')
image = tf.reshape(i, [1, 4, 5, 1], name='image')
res = tf.squeeze(tf.nn.conv2d(image, kernel, strides=[1, 1, 1, 1],
padding="VALID"))
# VALID means no padding
with tf.Session() as sess:
    print sess.run(res)
```

The output of the preceding listing is as follows--this is the same as the one we calculated manually:

```
[[ 3.  3.  3.]
 [ 2.  2.  4.]]
```

Strides

The primary purpose of convolutions is to reduce the dimensions of an image (width, height, and number of channels). The larger the image, the more processing time is required.

The `strides` parameter causes a kernel to skip over pixels in an image and not include them in the output. The `strides` parameter determines how a convolution operation works with a kernel when a larger image and more complex kernel are used. As a convolution is sliding the kernel over the input, it is using the `strides` parameter to determine how it walks over the input, instead of going over every element of an input.

Let's take a look at the following example, where we are moving a 3 x 3 x 1 kernel over a 6 x 6 x 1 image with a stride of 1, 3, 3, 1:

Step 1 as kernel slides with stride of 1,3,3,1

The kernel strides over the following elements in steps 3 and 4:

```
0.0 1.0 2.0 3.0 4.0 5.0
0.1 1.1 2.1 3.1 4.1 5.1
0.2 1.2 2.2 3.2 4.2 5.2
0.3 1.3 2.3 3.3 4.3 5.3
0.4 1.4 2.4 3.4 4.4 5.4
0.5 1.5 2.5 3.5 4.5 5.5

0.0 1.0 2.0 3.0 4.0 5.0
0.1 1.1 2.1 3.1 4.1 5.1
0.2 1.2 2.2 3.2 4.2 5.2
0.3 1.3 2.3 3.3 4.3 5.3
0.4 1.4 2.4 3.4 4.4 5.4
0.5 1.5 2.5 3.5 4.5 5.5
```

Step 3 and 4 of kernel stride over input

Let's implement this in TensorFlow; the output will be a 4 x 4 x 1 tensor:

```python
import tensorflow as tf

def main():
    session = tf.InteractiveSession()
    input_batch = tf.constant([
        [ # First Input  (6x6x1)
            [[0.0], [1.0], [2.0], [3.0], [4.0], [5.0]],
            [[0.1], [1.1], [2.1], [3.1], [4.1], [5.1]],
            [[0.2], [1.2], [2.2], [3.2], [4.2], [5.2]],
            [[0.3], [1.3], [2.3], [3.3], [4.3], [5.3]],
            [[0.4], [1.4], [2.4], [3.4], [4.4], [5.4]],
            [[0.5], [1.5], [2.5], [3.5], [4.5], [5.5]],
        ],
    ])
    kernel = tf.constant([ # Kernel (3x3x1)
        [[[0.0]], [[0.5]], [[0.0]]],
        [[[0.0]], [[0.5]], [[0.0]]],
        [[[0.0]], [[0.5]], [[0.0]]]
    ])

    # NOTE: the change in the size of the strides parameter.
    conv2d = tf.nn.conv2d(input_batch, kernel, strides=[1, 3, 3, 1],
    padding='SAME')
    conv2d_output = session.run(conv2d)
    print(conv2d_output)
    if __name__ == '__main__':
    main()
```

The output is similar to the following listing, in which 1, 3, 3, 1 stride leaders to four red boxes in the preceding image are being multiplied with the kernel:

```
[[[[ 1.64999998][ 6.1500001 ]]
  [[ 2.0999999 ][ 6.60000038]]]]
```

Pooling

Pooling layers help with overfitting and improve performance by reducing the size of the input tensor. Typically, they are used to scale down the input, keeping important information. Pooling is a much faster mechanism for input size reduction compared with `tf.nn.conv2d`.

The following pooling mechanisms are supported by TensorFlow:

- Average
- Max
- Max with argmax

Each pooling operation uses rectangular windows of size `ksize` separated by offset `strides`. If `strides` are all ones (1, 1, 1, 1), every window is used; if `strides` are all twos (1, 2, 2, 1), every other window is used in each dimension; and so on.

Max pool

The following defined function provides max pooling for the input 4D tensor `tf.nn.max_pool`:

```
max_pool(
    value, ksize, strides, padding, data_format='NHWC', name=None
)
```

The preceding arguments are explained here:

- `value`: This is the 4D tensor with shape [batch, height, width, channels], type `tf.float32` on which max pooling needs to be done.
- `ksize`: This is the list of ints that has `length >= 4`. The size of the window for each dimension of the input tensor.
- `strides`: This is the list of ints, `length >= 4`. A stride of the sliding window for each dimension of the input tensor.

- `padding`: This is a string, either `VALID` or `SAME`. The padding algorithm. The following section explains `VALID` and `SAME` padding.

- `"VALID"` = without padding:

```
    inputs:         1  2  3  4  5  6  7  8  9  10 11 (12 13)
                    |_____|              dropped
                          |_____|
```

- `"SAME"` = with zero padding:

```
                 pad|                              |pad
    inputs:        0 |1  2  3  4  5  6  7  8  9  10 11 12 13|0  0
                    |_____|
                          |_____|
                                |_____|
```

In this example:

- Input width = 13
- Filter width = 6
- Stride = 5

Reference: `https://stackoverflow.com/questions/37674306/what-is-the-difference-between-same-and-valid-padding-in-tf-nn-max-pool-of-t`

- `data_format`: This is a string. `NHWC` and `NCHW` are supported.
- `name`: This is the optional name for the operation.

Example code

The following code demonstrates max pooling on a tensor using a `VALID` padding scheme:

```
import tensorflow as tf

batch_size=1
input_height = 3
input_width = 3
input_channels = 1

def main():
  sess = tf.InteractiveSession()
```

```
layer_input = tf.constant([
  [
    [[1.0], [0.2], [2.0]],
    [[0.1], [1.2], [1.4]],
    [[1.1], [0.4], [0.4]]
  ]
])

# The strides will look at the entire input by using the image_height and
image_width
kernel = [batch_size, input_height, input_width, input_channels]
max_pool = tf.nn.max_pool(layer_input, kernel, [1, 1, 1, 1], "VALID")
print(sess.run(max_pool))

if __name__ == '__main__':
  main()
```

The output of the preceding listing will give the maximum values in the window 3 x 3 x 1:

```
[[[[ 2.]]]]
```

The following diagram explains how max pool logic works:

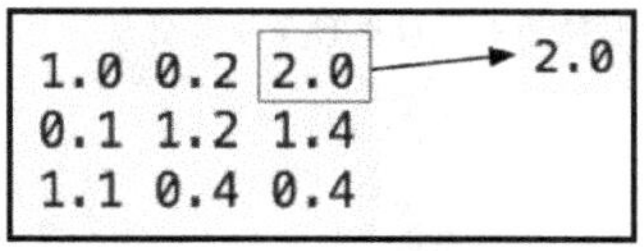

```
1.0 0.2 [2.0]━━━▶ 2.0
0.1 1.2 1.4
1.1 0.4 0.4
```

As can be seen, max pool selected the maximum value from the window based on a stride of 1, 1, 1.

Average pool

It performs the average pooling on the input tensor. Each entry in the output is the mean of the corresponding size `ksize` window in value. It is defined using the `tf.nn.avg_pool` method:

```
avg_pool( value, ksize, strides, padding, data_format='NHWC', name=None)
```

Let's look at the code example where `avg_pool` is used in a simple 2D tensor:

```
import tensorflow as tf

batch_size=1
input_height = 3
input_width = 3
```

```
input_channels = 1

def main():
  sess = tf.InteractiveSession()
  layer_input = tf.constant([
    [
      [[1.0], [0.2], [2.0]],
      [[0.1], [1.2], [1.4]],
      [[1.1], [0.4], [0.4]]
    ]
  ])

  # The strides will look at the entire input by using the image_height and
image_width
  kernel = [batch_size, input_height, input_width, input_channels]
  avg_pool = tf.nn.avg_pool(layer_input, kernel, [1, 1, 1, 1], "VALID")
  print(sess.run(avg_pool))

if __name__ == '__main__':
    main()
```

The output of the preceding listing is the average of all the values in the tensor.

$$Average = (1.0 + 0.2 + 2.0 + 0.1 + 1.2 + 1.4 + 1.1 + 0.4 + 0.4) / 9 = 0.86666$$

```
[[[[ 0.86666667]]]]
```

Image classification with convolutional networks

Let's look at a more realistic case for using CNNs; we will use the Stanford Dogs versus Cats dataset. This dataset has 100+ images of dogs and cats.

 You can download this dataset (100 images each) from the following location:
`https://s3.amazonaws.com/neural-networking-book/ch04/dogs_vs_cat s.tar.gz`

1. Import the relevant functions and Python classes:

```
import matplotlib.pyplot as plt
import tensorflow as tf
import pandas as pd
import numpy as np
```

```
from sklearn.metrics import confusion_matrix
import time
from datetime import timedelta
import math
import dataset
import random
```

2. We will define the parameters for the convolution layers. There are three
   convolution layers with the following parameters:

Layer number	Layer type	Number of filters/neurons
1	Convolution	32 filters
2	Convolution	32 filters
3	Convolution	64 filters
4	Fully connected	128 neurons

The Network topolgy can be represented as shown in the following diagram:

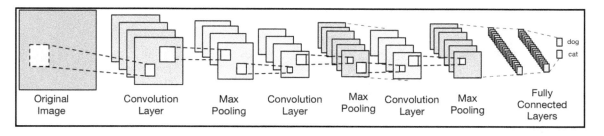

The following code should be helpful for understanding the parameters:

```
# Convolutional Layer 1.
filter_size1 = 3
num_filters1 = 32

# Convolutional Layer 2.
filter_size2 = 3
num_filters2 = 32

# Convolutional Layer 3.
filter_size3 = 3
num_filters3 = 64

# Fully-connected layer.
# Number of neurons in fully-connected layer.
```

```
fc_size = 128

# Number of color channels for the images: 1 channel for gray-
scale.
num_channels = 3

# image dimensions (only squares for now)
img_size = 128

# Size of image when flattened to a single dimension
img_size_flat = img_size * img_size * num_channels

# Tuple with height and width of images used to reshape arrays.
img_shape = (img_size, img_size)
```

3. Define the constant for the number of classes (two, in this case) and other variables. We have taken the Stanford dataset and reduced it to 100 images each of dogs and cats for easier processing:

```
# class info
classes = ['dogs', 'cats']
num_classes = len(classes)

# batch size
batch_size = 2

# validation split
validation_size = .2
total_iterations = 0
early_stopping = None   # use None if you don't want to implement
early stoping
home = '/home/ubuntu/Downloads/dogs_vs_cats'
train_path = home + '/train-cat-dog-100/'
test_path = home + '/test-cat-dog-100/'
checkpoint_dir = home + "/models/"
```

Let's first read the dataset into a tensor. The logic for the reading is defined in the dataset class:

```
data = dataset.read_train_sets(train_path, img_size, classes,
validation_size=validation_size)
```

Here, `train_path`, `image_size`, `classes`, and `validation_size` are defined. Let's look at the implementation of `read_train_sets(..)`:

```
def read_train_sets(train_path, image_size, classes,
validation_size=0):
```

```
class DataSets(object):
  pass
data_sets = DataSets()

  images, labels, ids, cls = load_train(train_path, image_size,
classes)
  images, labels, ids, cls = shuffle(images, labels, ids, cls)  #
shuffle the data

  if isinstance(validation_size, float):
    validation_size = int(validation_size * images.shape[0])

  validation_images = images[:validation_size]
  validation_labels = labels[:validation_size]
  validation_ids = ids[:validation_size]
  validation_cls = cls[:validation_size]

  train_images = images[validation_size:]
  train_labels = labels[validation_size:]
  train_ids = ids[validation_size:]
  train_cls = cls[validation_size:]

  data_sets.train = DataSet(train_images, train_labels, train_ids,
train_cls)
  data_sets.valid = DataSet(validation_images, validation_labels,
validation_ids,
    validation_cls)

  return data_sets
```

This method, in turn, calls `load_train(...)` to return a `numpy.array` of the data types:

```
def load_train(train_path, image_size, classes) :
 images = labels = []
 ids = cls = []
 # load data into arrays
 images = np.array(images)
 labels = np.array(labels)
 ids = np.array(ids)
 cls =  np.array(cls)
 return images, labels, ids, cls
```

The data loaded into training is a function of `validation_set`; it is calculated from the images array's first dimension:

```
+ (Ctrl+F1) images.shape = {tuple} <type 'tuple'>: (291, 128, 128, 3)
```

We calculate `validation_size` as shown in the following code:

```
validation_size = int(validation_size * images.shape[0])
```

As we have kept validation size as `0.2`, it comes out to `58.2` rounded off to `58`:

```
validation_size = (int) 58
```

Similarly, we create the test dataset, `test_images` and `test_ids`:

```
test_images, test_ids = dataset.read_test_set(test_path, img_size)
```

Here, `read_test_set(...)` is a function called internally:

```
def read_test_set(test_path, image_size):
    images, ids  = load_test(test_path, image_size)
    return images, ids
```

`read_test_set(test_path, image_size)` in turn calls `load_test(test_path, image_size)`, for which the listing is given as follows:

```
def load_test(test_path, image_size):
    path = os.path.join(test_path, '*g')
    files = sorted(glob.glob(path))

    X_test = []
    X_test_id = []
    print("Reading test images")
    for fl in files:
        flbase = os.path.basename(fl)
        img = cv2.imread(fl)
        img = cv2.resize(img, (image_size, image_size), fx=0.5,
fy=0.5,
            interpolation=cv2.INTER_LINEAR)

        #img = cv2.resize(img, (image_size, image_size),
cv2.INTER_LINEAR)
        X_test.append(img)
        X_test_id.append(flbase)

    ### because we're not creating a DataSet object for the test
images,
    ### normalization happens here
    X_test = np.array(X_test, dtype=np.uint8)
    X_test = X_test.astype('float32')
    X_test = X_test / 255
```

```
       return X_test, X_test_id
```

4. Let's look at the sizes of the various `numpy` arrays created:

```
print("Size of:")
print("- Training-set:\t\t{}".format(len(data.train.labels)))
print("- Test-set:\t\t{}".format(len(test_images)))
print("- Validation-set:\t{}".format(len(data.valid.labels)))

Size of:Size of:
- Training-set: 233
- Test-set: 100
- Validation-set: 58
```

5. Plot nine random images in a grid of 3 x 3 with the appropriate classes:

```
images, cls_true = data.train.images, data.train.cls
plot_images(images=images, cls_true=cls_true
```

Here, the `plot_images` function is defined in the following code block:

```
def plot_images(images, cls_true, cls_pred=None):
    if len(images) == 0:
        print("no images to show")
        return
    else:
        random_indices = random.sample(range(len(images)),
min(len(images), 9))
        images, cls_true = zip(*[(images[i], cls_true[i]) for i in
random_indices])
    # Create figure with 3x3 sub-plots.
    fig, axes = plt.subplots(3, 3)
    fig.subplots_adjust(hspace=0.3, wspace=0.3)

    for i, ax in enumerate(axes.flat):
        # Plot image.
        print(images[i])
        ax.imshow(images[i].reshape(img_size, img_size,
num_channels))
        print(images[i].size)
        print(img_size)
        print(num_channels)
        # Show true and predicted classes.
        if cls_pred is None:
            xlabel = "True: {0}".format(cls_true[i])
        else:
            xlabel = "True: {0}, Pred: {1}".format(cls_true[i],
cls_pred[i])
```

```
# Show the classes as the label on the x-axis.
ax.set_xlabel(xlabel)
# Remove ticks from the plot.
ax.set_xticks([])
ax.set_yticks([])
# Ensure the plot is shown correctly with multiple plots
# in a single Notebook cell.
plt.show()
```

The following is the output of our code:

Nine random images from the dataset

Defining a tensor for input images and the first convolution layer

Next, we will define a tensor for input images and the first convolution layer.

Input tensor

Create a placeholder with `shape[None, img_size_flat]` and reshape it into `[-1, img_size, img_size, num_channels]`:

```
x = tf.placeholder(tf.float32, shape=[None, img_size_flat], name='x')
x_image = tf.reshape(x, [-1, img_size, img_size, num_channels])
```

Here, the parameters `img_size` and `num_channels` have the following values:

- `img_size` = 128
- `num_channels` = 3

First convolution layer

After reshaping the input tensor into `x_image`, we will create the first convolution layer:

```
layer_conv1, weights_conv1 = new_conv_layer(input=x_image,
num_input_channels=num_channels,
                                        filter_size=filter_size1,
                                        num_filters=num_filters1,
                                        use_pooling=True)
print(layer_conv1)
```

The `new_conv_layer(...)` function is defined here. Let's look at the value of each variable being sent to this function:

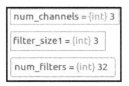

```
def new_conv_layer(input,                # The previous layer.
                num_input_channels,  # Num. channels in prev. layer.
                filter_size,         # Width and height of each filter.
                num_filters,         # Number of filters.
                use_pooling=True):   # Use 2x2 max-pooling.

    # Shape of the filter-weights for the convolution.
    # This format is determined by the TensorFlow API.
    shape = [filter_size, filter_size, num_input_channels, num_filters]

    # Create new weights aka. filters with the given shape.
    weights = new_weights(shape=shape)
```

```
# Create new biases, one for each filter.
biases = new_biases(length=num_filters)

# Create the TensorFlow operation for convolution.
# Note the strides are set to 1 in all dimensions.
# The first and last stride must always be 1,
# because the first is for the image-number and
# the last is for the input-channel.
# But e.g. strides=[1, 2, 2, 1] would mean that the filter
# is moved 2 pixels across the x- and y-axis of the image.
# The padding is set to 'SAME' which means the input image
# is padded with zeroes so the size of the output is the same.
layer = tf.nn.conv2d(input=input,
                     filter=weights,
                     strides=[1, 1, 1, 1],
                     padding='SAME')

# Add the biases to the results of the convolution.
# A bias-value is added to each filter-channel.
layer += biases

# Use pooling to down-sample the image resolution?
if use_pooling:
    # This is 2x2 max-pooling, which means that we
    # consider 2x2 windows and select the largest value
    # in each window. Then we move 2 pixels to the next window.
    layer = tf.nn.max_pool(value=layer,
                           ksize=[1, 2, 2, 1],
                           strides=[1, 2, 2, 1],
                           padding='SAME')

# Rectified Linear Unit (ReLU).
# It calculates max(x, 0) for each input pixel x.
# This adds some non-linearity to the formula and allows us
# to learn more complicated functions.
layer = tf.nn.relu(layer)

# Note that ReLU is normally executed before the pooling,
# but since relu(max_pool(x)) == max_pool(relu(x)) we can
# save 75% of the relu-operations by max-pooling first.

# We return both the resulting layer and the filter-weights
# because we will plot the weights later.
return layer, weights
```

The variables have the following values at runtime:

+ (Ctrl+F1) biases = {Variable} <tf.Variable 'Variable_1:0' shape=(32,) dtype=float32_ref>

+ (Ctrl+F1) weights = {Variable} <tf.Variable 'Variable:0' shape=(3, 3, 3, 32) dtype=float32_ref>

If we run this, the output of the `print (..)` statement will be as follows:

```
Tensor("Relu:0", shape=(?, 64, 64, 32), dtype=float32)
```

The output shows the shape of the output tensor coming out of input layer 1.

Second convolution layer

In the second convolution layer, we start with the first layer's output as input and build a new layer with the following parameters:

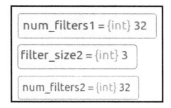

First, we define a placeholder for real y and the class of real y (the label of the class):

```
y_true = tf.placeholder(tf.float32, shape=[None, num_classes],
name='y_true')

y_true_cls = tf.argmax(y_true, dimension=1)
```

The shape of these two variables is the following:

+ (Ctrl+F1) y_true = {Tensor} Tensor("y_true:0", shape=(?, 2), dtype=float32)

+ (Ctrl+F1) y_true_cls = {Tensor} Tensor("ArgMax:0", shape=(?,), dtype=int64)

```
layer_conv2, weights_conv2 = new_conv_layer(input=layer_conv1,
num_input_channels=num_filters1, filter_size=filter_size2, num_filters=num_fi
```

```
lters2,use_pooling=True)
```

where following are the values:

- `num_input_channels` = 3
- `filter_size` = 3
- `num_filters` = 32

This is the output of the printout:

```
Tensor("Relu_1:0", shape=(?, 32, 32, 32), dtype=float32)
```

Third convolution layer

This layer takes the output of the second layer as the input. Let's look at the inputs going into the creation of this layer:

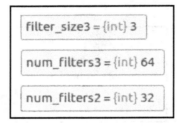

```
shape = [filter_size, filter_size, num_input_channels, num_filters] weights
= new_weights(shape=shape)

layer_conv3, weights_conv3 = new_conv_layer(input=layer_conv2,
num_input_channels=num_filters2,filter_size=filter_size3,num_filters=num_fi
lters3,use_pooling=True)

print(layer_conv3)
```

The shape of `layer_conv3` is as follows:

```
Tensor("Relu_2:0", shape=(?, 16, 16, 64), dtype=float32)
```

Flatten the layer

Next, we flatten the layer to the num of images and the num of features, which is 16,384 in this case. If you notice for the last layer's output, we have flattened it with the following logic, 16 x 16 x 64 = 16,384:

```
layer_flat, num_features = flatten_layer(layer_conv3)
```

If we print these values, you will see the following output:

```
Tensor("Reshape_1:0", shape=(?, 16384), dtype=float32)
16384
```

Fully connected layers

In the fourth and fifth layers, we define fully connected layers:

```
layer_fc1 = new_fc_layer(input=layer_flat,
                         num_inputs=num_features,
                         num_outputs=fc_size,
                         use_relu=True)
```

where

- `layer_flat`: the last layer flattened
- `num_features`: number of features
- `fc_size`: number of outputs

The following image shows the values that are passed to `new_fc_layer()`:

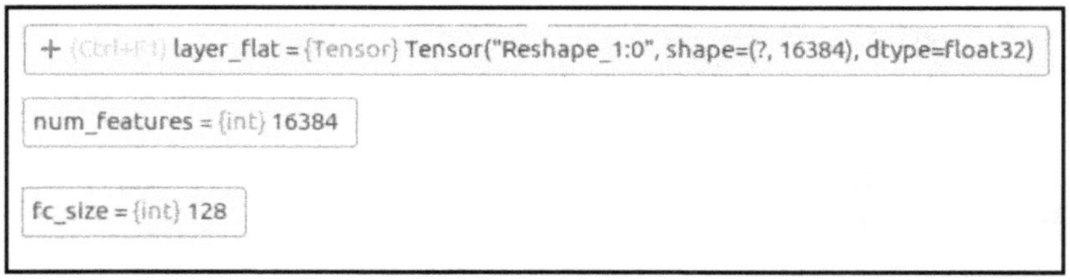

```
print(layer_fc1)
```

The value of the print is as follows:

```
Tensor("Relu_3:0", shape=(?, 128), dtype=float32)
```

Next is the fully connected layer 2, where the function takes the following parameters:

- `layer_fc1`: the output from the first fully connected layer
- `num_inputs`: 128
- `num_inputs`: `num_classes`, 2 in this case
- `use_relu`: a Boolean function specifying whether to use `relu` or not; `False` in this case

```
layer_fc2 = new_fc_layer(input=layer_fc1,
                         num_inputs=fc_size,
                         num_outputs=num_classes,
                         use_relu=False)
```

Let's take a look at the output of the second fully connected layer:

```
print(layer_fc2)

Tensor("add_4:0", shape=(?, 2), dtype=float32)
```

Defining cost and optimizer

Apply Softmax on the output from `layer_fc2` (the fully connected second layer).

In mathematics, the `softmax` function, or normalized exponential function, [1]:198 is a generalization of the `logistic function` that *squashes* a K-dimensional vector Z of arbitrary real values to a K-dimensional vector $\sigma(z)$ of real values in the range [0, 1] that add up to *1*. The function is given by the following formula:

$$\sigma(\mathbf{z})_j = \frac{e^{z_j}}{\sum_{k=1}^{K} e^{z_k}} \quad \text{for } j = 1, ..., K.$$

```
y_pred = tf.nn.softmax(layer_fc2)
y_pred_cls = tf.argmax(y_pred, dimension=1)
```

Calculate the cross entropy:

```
cross_entropy = tf.nn.softmax_cross_entropy_with_logits(
   logits=layer_fc2,
   labels=y_true)
cost = tf.reduce_mean(cross_entropy)
```

Optimizer

Next, we define the optimizer, which is based on the Adam optimizer.

Adam is different to the stochastic gradient descent algorithm. Stochastic gradient descent maintains a single learning rate (called **alpha**) for all weight updates and the learning rate does not change during training.

This algorithm maintains a learning rate for each network weight (parameter) and separately adapts as learning unfolds. It computes individual adaptive learning rates for different parameters from the estimates of the first and second moments of the gradients.

Adam combines the advantages of two other extensions of stochastic gradient descent.

The **adaptive gradient algorithm** (**AdaGrad**) maintains a per-parameter learning rate that improves performance for ML problems with sparse gradients (for example, natural language and computer vision problems). **Root mean square propagation** (**RMSProp**) maintains learning rates for each parameter; these are adapted based on the average of recent values of the gradients for the weight (how quickly it is changing).

```
optimizer = tf.train.AdamOptimizer(learning_rate=1e-4).minimize(cost)
```

We also calculate the variables for `correct_prediction` and `accuracy`:

```
correct_prediction = tf.equal(y_pred_cls, y_true_cls)
accuracy = tf.reduce_mean(tf.cast(correct_prediction, tf.float32))
```

First epoch

Initialize the session and call the `optimize()` function for `num_iterations=1`:

```
session = tf.Session()
session.run(tf.global_variables_initializer())
batch_size = 2
train_batch_size = batch_size
optimize(num_iterations = 1, data=data, train_batch_size=train_batch_size,
x=x, y_true=y_true,
session=session, optimizer=optimizer, cost=cost, accuracy=accuracy)
```

Here, the `optimize()` function is defined in the following block:

```
def optimize(num_iterations, data, train_batch_size, x, y_true, session,
optimizer, cost, accuracy):
    # Ensure we update the global variable rather than a local copy.
    global total_iterations

    # Start-time used for printing time-usage below.
    start_time = time.time()
    best_val_loss = float("inf")
    patience = 0

    for i in range(total_iterations,
                   total_iterations + num_iterations):

        # Get a batch of training examples.
        # x_batch now holds a batch of images and
        # y_true_batch are the true labels for those images.
        x_batch, y_true_batch, _, cls_batch =
data.train.next_batch(train_batch_size)
        x_valid_batch, y_valid_batch, _, valid_cls_batch =
data.valid.next_batch(train_batch_size)

        # Convert shape from [num examples, rows, columns, depth]
        # to [num examples, flattened image shape]

        x_batch = x_batch.reshape(train_batch_size, img_size_flat)
        x_valid_batch = x_valid_batch.reshape(train_batch_size,
img_size_flat)

        # Put the batch into a dict with the proper names
        # for placeholder variables in the TensorFlow graph.
        feed_dict_train = {x: x_batch,
                           y_true: y_true_batch}
        feed_dict_validate = {x: x_valid_batch,
                              y_true: y_valid_batch}

        # Run the optimizer using this batch of training data.
        # TensorFlow assigns the variables in feed_dict_train
        # to the placeholder variables and then runs the optimizer.
        session.run(optimizer, feed_dict=feed_dict_train)
        # Print status at end of each epoch (defined as full pass through
        # training dataset).
        if i % int(data.train.num_examples/batch_size) == 0:
            val_loss = session.run(cost, feed_dict=feed_dict_validate)
            epoch = int(i / int(data.train.num_examples/batch_size))
            #print_progress(epoch, feed_dict_train, feed_dict_validate,
val_loss)
```

```
            print_progress(session, accuracy, epoch, feed_dict_train,
feed_dict_validate,
                val_loss)
            if early_stopping:
                if val_loss < best_val_loss:
                    best_val_loss = val_loss
                    patience = 0
                else:
                    patience += 1

                if patience == early_stopping:
                    break

    # Update the total number of iterations performed.
    total_iterations += num_iterations

    # Ending time.
    end_time = time.time()

    # Difference between start and end-times.
    time_dif = end_time - start_time

    # Print the time-usage.
    print("Time elapsed: " + str(timedelta(seconds=int(round(time_dif)))))
```

The output that prints the training, validation accuracy, and validation loss is listed here:

```
Epoch 1 --- Training Accuracy: 100.0%, Validation Accuracy: 50.0%,
Validation Loss: 0.705
```

Print the accuracy of `Test-Set`:

```
print_validation_accuracy(x, y_true, y_pred_cls, session, data,
show_example_errors=True, show_confusion_matrix=False)
Epoch 2 --- Training Accuracy: 50.0%, Validation Accuracy: 100.0%,
Validation Loss: 0.320
Accuracy on Test-Set: 43.1% (25 / 58)
```

Next, let's optimize the model for `100` iterations:

```
optimize(num_iterations=100, data=data, train_batch_size=train_batch_size,
x=x, y_true=y_true,session=session, optimizer=optimizer, cost=cost,
accuracy=accuracy)

print_validation_accuracy(x, y_true, y_pred_cls, session, data,
show_example_errors=True,
                            show_confusion_matrix=False)
Accuracy on Test-Set: 62.1% (36 / 58)
```

The output also shows false positives:

True: cats, Pred: dogs   True: cats, Pred: dogs   True: cats, Pred: dogs

True: cats, Pred: dogs   True: cats, Pred: dogs   True: cats, Pred: dogs

True: cats, Pred: dogs   True: cats, Pred: dogs   True: cats, Pred: dogs

Output showing false positives

Plotting filters and their effects on an image

Let's apply filters in two layers to two test images and see how that affects them:

```
image1 = test_images[0]
plot_image(image1)
```

The output of the `plot_image(image1)` function is shown in the following image:

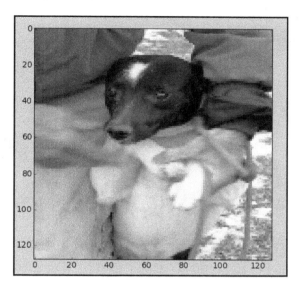

```
image2 = test_images[13]
plot_image(image2)
```

The output of `image2` with filters applied is shown here:

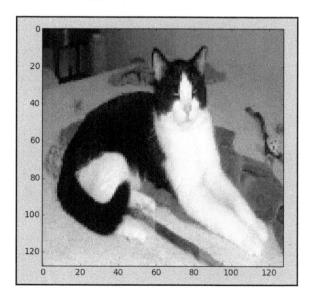

Convolution layer 1: The following is the plot for weights for layer 1:

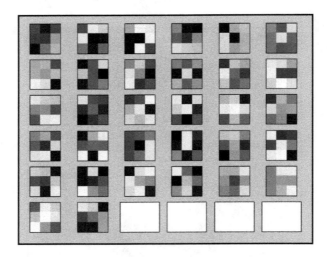

Filters from layer 1 applied to i mage 1:

```
plot_conv_layer(layer=layer_conv1, image=image1, session=session, x=x)
```

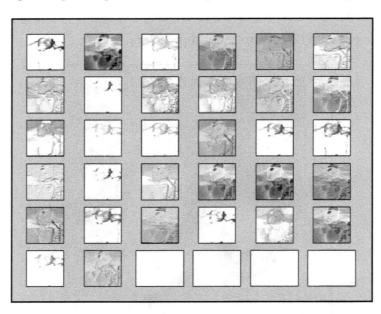

Filters from Layer 1 applied to Image 2:

```
plot_conv_layer(layer=layer_conv1, image=image2, session=session, x=x)
```

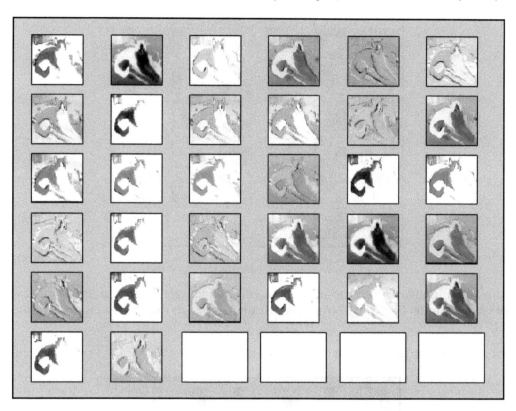

Convolution layer 2: Now plot the filter-weights for the second convolutional layer. There are 16 output channels from the first conv-layer, which means there are 16 input channels to the second conv-layer. The second Conv layer has a set of filter-weights for each of its input channels. We start by plotting the filter-weights for the first channel.

Layer 2 weights:

```
plot_conv_weights(weights=weights_conv1, session=session)
```

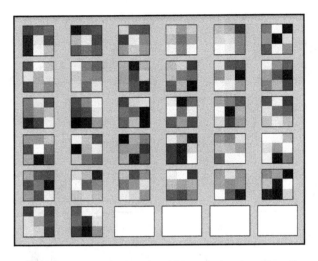

Weights for Conv2, input channel 0. Positive weights are red and negative weights are blue

There are 16 input channels to the second convolutional layer, so we can make another 15 plots of filter-weights like this. We just make one more with the filter-weights for the second channel:

```
plot_conv_weights(weights=weights_conv2, session=session, input_channel=1)
```

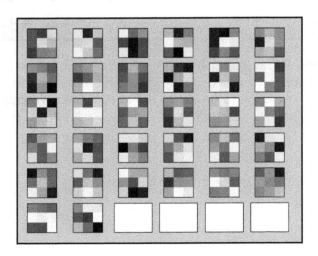

Positive weights are red and negative weights are blue

Plot Images 1 and 2 with filters from convolution layer 2:

```
plot_conv_layer(layer=layer_conv2, image=image1, session=session, x=x)
plot_conv_layer(layer=layer_conv2, image=image2, session=session, x=x)
```

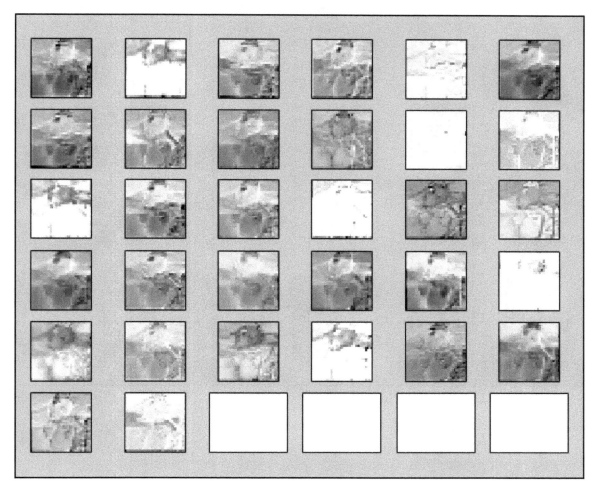

Weights for conv2, input channel 1. Image displaying image1 filtered through a layer 2 filter

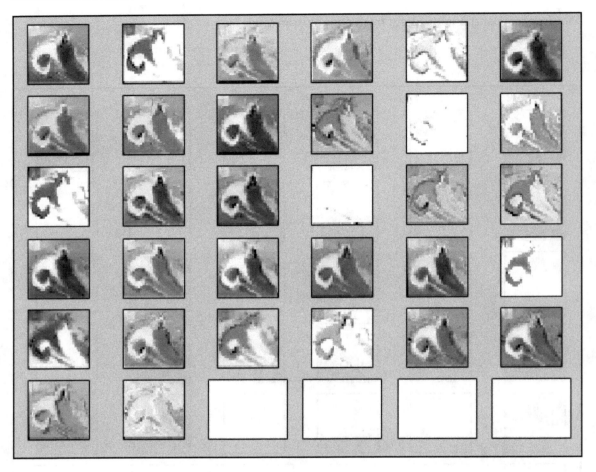

Image displaying image 2 filtered through a layer 2 filter

Convolution Layer 3: Let's print the layer 3 weights; this layer has 64 filters. This is how images 1 and 2 look passed through each of these filters:

```
plot_conv_weights(weights=weights_conv3, session=session, input_channel=0)
```

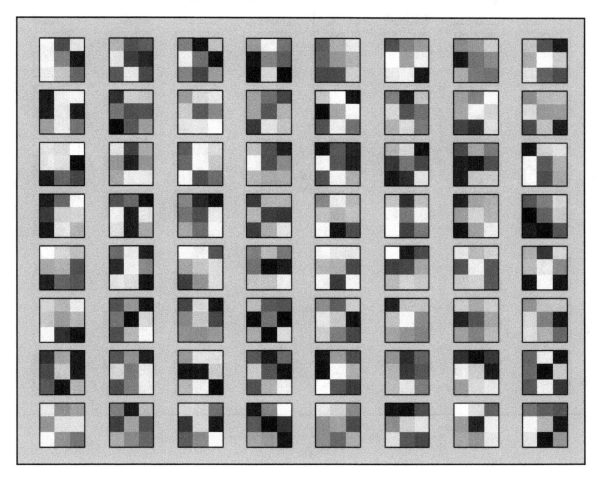

Weights for Conv2, Input Channel 0, Positive weights are red and negative weights are blue

```
plot_conv_weights(weights=weights_conv3, session=session, input_channel=1)
```

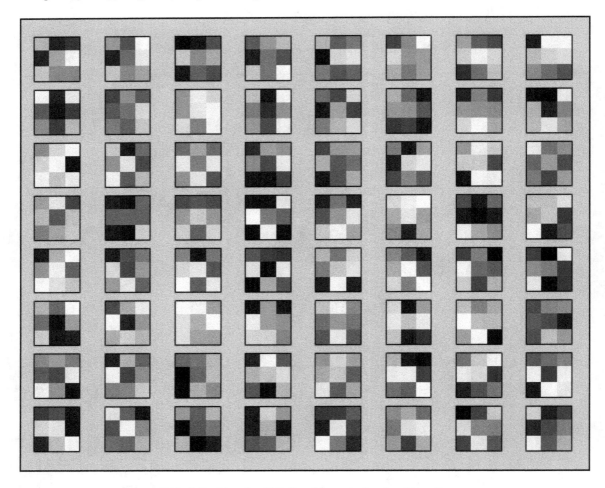

Weights for Conv2, input channel 1. Positive weights are red and negative weights are blue.

Plotting an image passed through layer 3 filters: Execute the following statements to plot images 1 and 2 being passed from 64 filters of convolution layer 3:

```
plot_conv_layer(layer=layer_conv3, image=image1, session=session, x=x)
plot_conv_layer(layer=layer_conv3, image=image2, session=session, x=x)
```

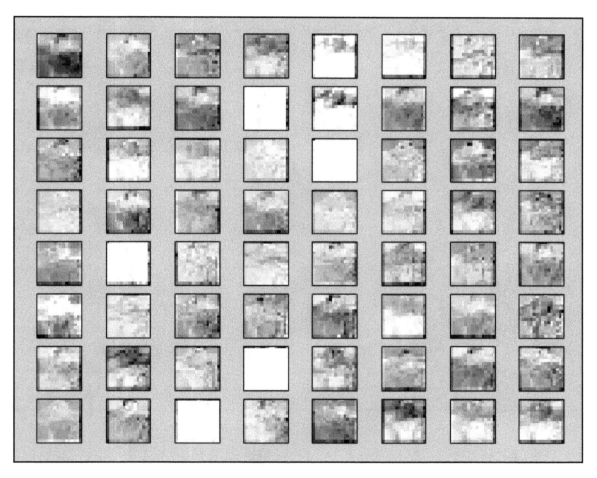

Image 1, plotted with convolution filters from conv3

The following is the image with convolution filters from conv3:

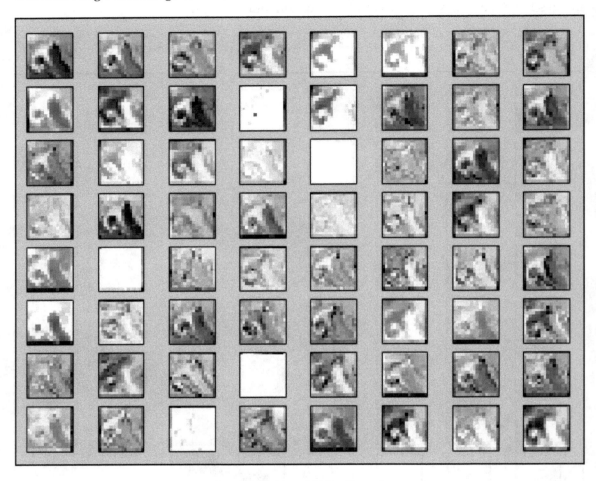

Image 2, plotted with convolution filters from conv3

With this, we have completed the analysis of the Cats versus Dogs dataset, where we used a five-layer CNN with three hidden layers and two fully connected layers to build our model.

Summary

In this chapter, you learned the basics of convolution and why it is an effective mechanism for image label prediction. You learned about basic concepts such as `strides` and padding. This was followed by an example based on the Stanford dataset of Cats versus Dogs. We used three convolution layers to build the neural network and two fully connected layers to showcase how it is used to classify the images. We also plotted the weights for three layers and saw how filters modify the image. We also looked at concepts such as image pooling and how it helps make CNN more efficient.

In the next chapter we look at a different kind of neural network called a **Recurrent Neural Network (RNN)**, which processes time series data or is used for **natural language processing (NLP)** to predict next word in a sequence

5
Recurrent Neural Networks

Recurrent Neural Networks (**RNNs**) make use of sequential or time series data. In a regular neural network, we consider that all inputs and outputs are independent of each other. For a task where you want to predict the next word in a given sentence, it's better to know which words have come before it. RNNs are recurrent as the same task is performed for every element in the sequence where the output is dependent on the previous calculations. RNNs can be thought of as having a **memory** that captures information about what has been computed so far.

Going from feedforward neural networks to recurrent neural networks, we will use the concept of sharing parameters across various parts of the model. Parameter sharing will make it possible to extend and apply the model to examples of different forms (different lengths, here) and generalize across them.

Introduction to RNNs

To understand RNNs, we have to understand the basics of feedforward neural networks. You can refer to `Chapter 3`, *Optimization for Neural Networks*, for details on feedforward networks. Both feedforward and recurrent neural networks are identified from the way they process the information or features through a series of mathematical operations performed at the various nodes of the network. One feeds information straight through (never touching a given node twice), the other cycles it through a loop.

A feedforward neural network is trained on image data until it minimizes the loss or error while predicting or classifying the categories for image types. With the trained set of hyper parameters or weights, the neural network can classify data it has never seen before. A trained feedforward neural network can be shown any random collection of images and the first image it classifies will not alter how it classifies the other images.

In a nutshell, these networks have no notion of order in time or temporal pattern, and the only information they consider is the current example it has been asked to classify.

RNNs take into account the temporal nature of the input data. An input to the RNN cell is both from the current timestep and one step back in time. Details are presented in the following diagram:

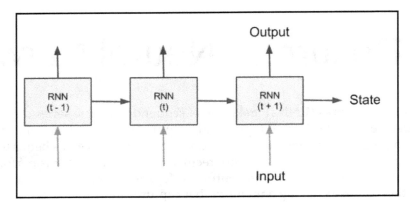

RNNs are recurrent in nature because they perform the same computation for every element in a sequence where the output is dependent on the previous computations. The other way to think about RNNs is that they have memory that can capture the information about what has been computed so far. RNNs can make use of the information or knowledge in long sequences but practically they are restricted to looking back only a few steps.

A typical RNN looks as follows:

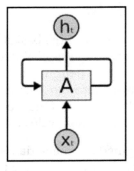

An unwrapped version of the RNN is shown in the following image; by unwrapping we mean that we write out the neural network for a complete sequence. Consider a sequence of five words; the network will be unwrapped into a five-layer neural network, one layer for each word:

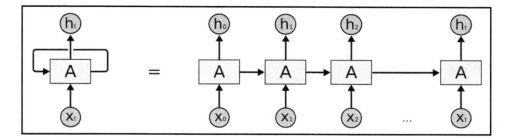

Computations happening in an RNN are as follows:

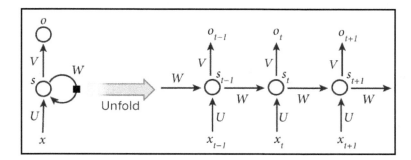

- x_t denotes the input at timestep t.

- s_t denotes the hidden state at timestep t. The hidden state is the memory of the network. s_t is computed based on the previously hidden state and the input at the current step, $s_t = f(Ux_t + Ws_{t-1})$.

- Function f represents non-linearity such as *tanh* or ReLU. The first hidden state is typically initialized to all zeroes.

- o_t denotes the output at step t. To predict the next word in a given sentence, it will be a vector of probabilities across the vocabulary, $o_t = \text{softmax}(Vs_t)$.

RNN implementation

Following program processes, a sequence of numbers and the goal is to predict the next value, with the previous values provided. The input to the RNN network at every time step is the current value and a state vector that represents or stores what the neural network has seen at timesteps before. This state-vector is the encoded memory of the RNN, initially set to zero.

Training data is basically a random binary vector. The output is shifted to the right.

```python
from __future__ import print_function, division
import tensorflow as tf
import numpy as np
import matplotlib.pyplot as plt


"""
define all the constants
"""
numEpochs = 10
seriesLength = 50000
backpropagationLength = 15
stateSize = 4
numClasses = 2
echoStep = 3
batchSize = 5
num_batches = seriesLength // batchSize // backpropagationLength


"""
generate data
"""
def generateData():
    x = np.array(np.random.choice(2, seriesLength, p=[0.5, 0.5]))
    y = np.roll(x, echoStep)
    y[0:echoStep] = 0

    x = x.reshape((batchSize, -1))
    y = y.reshape((batchSize, -1))

    return (x, y)


"""
start computational graph
"""
batchXHolder = tf.placeholder(tf.float32, [batchSize,
backpropagationLength], name="x_input")
batchYHolder = tf.placeholder(tf.int32, [batchSize, backpropagationLength],
name="y_input")

initState = tf.placeholder(tf.float32, [batchSize, stateSize],
"rnn_init_state")

W = tf.Variable(np.random.rand(stateSize+1, stateSize), dtype=tf.float32,
name="weight1")
bias1 = tf.Variable(np.zeros((1,stateSize)), dtype=tf.float32)
```

```
W2 = tf.Variable(np.random.rand(stateSize, numClasses),dtype=tf.float32,
name="weight2")
bias2 = tf.Variable(np.zeros((1,numClasses)), dtype=tf.float32)

tf.summary.histogram(name="weights", values=W)


# Unpack columns
inputsSeries = tf.unstack(batchXHolder, axis=1, name="input_series")
labelsSeries = tf.unstack(batchYHolder, axis=1, name="labels_series")


# Forward pass
currentState = initState
statesSeries = []
for currentInput in inputsSeries:
    currentInput = tf.reshape(currentInput, [batchSize, 1],
name="current_input")
    inputAndStateConcatenated = tf.concat([currentInput, currentState], 1,
name="input_state_concat")

    nextState = tf.tanh(tf.matmul(inputAndStateConcatenated, W) + bias1,
name="next_state")
    statesSeries.append(nextState)
    currentState = nextState


# calculate loss
logits_series = [tf.matmul(state, W2) + bias2 for state in statesSeries]
predictions_series = [tf.nn.softmax(logits) for logits in logits_series]

losses = [tf.nn.sparse_softmax_cross_entropy_with_logits(labels=labels,
logits=logits) for logits, labels in zip(logits_series,labelsSeries)]
total_loss = tf.reduce_mean(losses, name="total_loss")

train_step = tf.train.AdagradOptimizer(0.3).minimize(total_loss,
name="training")


"""
plot computation
"""
def plot(loss_list, predictions_series, batchX, batchY):
    plt.subplot(2, 3, 1)
    plt.cla()
    plt.plot(loss_list)

    for batchSeriesIdx in range(5):
```

```
            oneHotOutputSeries = np.array(predictions_series)[:,
batchSeriesIdx, :]
            singleOutputSeries = np.array([(1 if out[0] < 0.5 else 0) for out
in oneHotOutputSeries])

            plt.subplot(2, 3, batchSeriesIdx + 2)
            plt.cla()
            plt.axis([0, backpropagationLength, 0, 2])
            left_offset = range(backpropagationLength)
            plt.bar(left_offset, batchX[batchSeriesIdx, :], width=1,
color="blue")
            plt.bar(left_offset, batchY[batchSeriesIdx, :] * 0.5, width=1,
color="red")
            plt.bar(left_offset, singleOutputSeries * 0.3, width=1,
color="green")

    plt.draw()
    plt.pause(0.0001)


"""
run the graph
"""
with tf.Session() as sess:
    writer = tf.summary.FileWriter("logs", graph=tf.get_default_graph())
    sess.run(tf.global_variables_initializer())
    plt.ion()
    plt.figure()
    plt.show()
    loss_list = []

    for epoch_idx in range(numEpochs):
        x,y = generateData()
        _current_state = np.zeros((batchSize, stateSize))

        print("New data, epoch", epoch_idx)

        for batch_idx in range(num_batches):
            start_idx = batch_idx * backpropagationLength
            end_idx = start_idx + backpropagationLength

            batchX = x[:,start_idx:end_idx]
            batchY = y[:,start_idx:end_idx]

            _total_loss, _train_step, _current_state, _predictions_series =
sess.run(
                [total_loss, train_step, currentState, predictions_series],
                feed_dict={
```

```
                    batchXHolder:batchX,
                    batchYHolder:batchY,
                    initState:_current_state
                })

        loss_list.append(_total_loss)

        # fix the cost summary later
        tf.summary.scalar(name="totalloss", tensor=_total_loss)

        if batch_idx%100 == 0:
            print("Step",batch_idx, "Loss", _total_loss)
            plot(loss_list, _predictions_series, batchX, batchY)

plt.ioff()
plt.show()
```

Computational graph

The computational graph is shown as following:

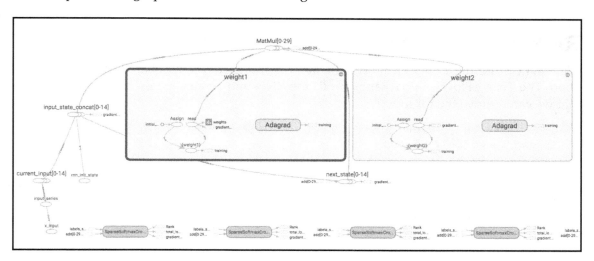

The output of the listing is shown as follows:

```
New data, epoch 0
Step 0 Loss 0.777418
Step 600 Loss 0.693907
New data, epoch 1
Step 0 Loss 0.690996
Step 600 Loss 0.691115
```

```
New data, epoch 2
Step 0 Loss 0.69259
Step 600 Loss 0.685826
New data, epoch 3
Step 0 Loss 0.684189
Step 600 Loss 0.690608
New data, epoch 4
Step 0 Loss 0.691302
Step 600 Loss 0.691309
New data, epoch 5
Step 0 Loss 0.69172
Step 600 Loss 0.694034
New data, epoch 6
Step 0 Loss 0.692927
Step 600 Loss 0.42796
New data, epoch 7
Step 0 Loss 0.42423
Step 600 Loss 0.00845207
New data, epoch 8
Step 0 Loss 0.188478
Step 500 Loss 0.00427217
```

RNN implementation with TensorFlow

We will now use the TensorFlow API; the inner workings of the RNN are hidden under the hood. The TensorFlow rnn package unrolls the RNN and creates the graph automatically so that we can remove the for loop:

```python
from __future__ import print_function, division
import tensorflow as tf
import numpy as np
import matplotlib.pyplot as plt

"""
define all the constants
"""
numEpochs = 10
seriesLength = 50000
backpropagationLength = 15
stateSize = 4
numClasses = 2
echoStep = 3
batchSize = 5
num_batches = seriesLength // batchSize // backpropagationLength
```

```
"""
generate data
"""
def generateData():
    x = np.array(np.random.choice(2, seriesLength, p=[0.5, 0.5]))
    y = np.roll(x, echoStep)
    y[0:echoStep] = 0

    x = x.reshape((batchSize, -1))
    y = y.reshape((batchSize, -1))

    return (x, y)


"""
start computational graph
"""
batchXHolder = tf.placeholder(tf.float32, [batchSize,
backpropagationLength], name="x_input")
batchYHolder = tf.placeholder(tf.int32, [batchSize, backpropagationLength],
name="y_input")

initState = tf.placeholder(tf.float32, [batchSize, stateSize],
"rnn_init_state")

W = tf.Variable(np.random.rand(stateSize+1, stateSize), dtype=tf.float32,
name="weight1")
bias1 = tf.Variable(np.zeros((1,stateSize)), dtype=tf.float32)

W2 = tf.Variable(np.random.rand(stateSize, numClasses),dtype=tf.float32,
name="weight2")
bias2 = tf.Variable(np.zeros((1,numClasses)), dtype=tf.float32)

tf.summary.histogram(name="weights", values=W)


# Unpack columns
inputsSeries = tf.split(axis=1, num_or_size_splits=backpropagationLength,
value=batchXHolder)
labelsSeries = tf.unstack(batchYHolder, axis=1)

# Forward passes
from tensorflow.contrib import rnn
cell = rnn.BasicRNNCell(stateSize)
statesSeries, currentState = rnn.static_rnn(cell, inputsSeries, initState)

# calculate loss
logits_series = [tf.matmul(state, W2) + bias2 for state in statesSeries]
```

```
predictions_series = [tf.nn.softmax(logits) for logits in logits_series]

losses = [tf.nn.sparse_softmax_cross_entropy_with_logits(labels=labels,
logits=logits) for logits, labels in zip(logits_series,labelsSeries)]
total_loss = tf.reduce_mean(losses, name="total_loss")

train_step = tf.train.AdagradOptimizer(0.3).minimize(total_loss,
name="training")


"""
plot computation
"""
def plot(loss_list, predictions_series, batchX, batchY):
    plt.subplot(2, 3, 1)
    plt.cla()
    plt.plot(loss_list)

    for batchSeriesIdx in range(5):
        oneHotOutputSeries = np.array(predictions_series)[:,
batchSeriesIdx, :]
        singleOutputSeries = np.array([(1 if out[0] < 0.5 else 0) for out
in oneHotOutputSeries])

        plt.subplot(2, 3, batchSeriesIdx + 2)
        plt.cla()
        plt.axis([0, backpropagationLength, 0, 2])
        left_offset = range(backpropagationLength)
        plt.bar(left_offset, batchX[batchSeriesIdx, :], width=1,
color="blue")
        plt.bar(left_offset, batchY[batchSeriesIdx, :] * 0.5, width=1,
color="red")
        plt.bar(left_offset, singleOutputSeries * 0.3, width=1,
color="green")

    plt.draw()
    plt.pause(0.0001)


"""
run the graph
"""
with tf.Session() as sess:
    writer = tf.summary.FileWriter("logs", graph=tf.get_default_graph())
    sess.run(tf.global_variables_initializer())
    plt.ion()
    plt.figure()
    plt.show()
```

```
    loss_list = []

    for epoch_idx in range(numEpochs):
        x,y = generateData()
        _current_state = np.zeros((batchSize, stateSize))

        print("New data, epoch", epoch_idx)

        for batch_idx in range(num_batches):
            start_idx = batch_idx * backpropagationLength
            end_idx = start_idx + backpropagationLength

            batchX = x[:,start_idx:end_idx]
            batchY = y[:,start_idx:end_idx]

            _total_loss, _train_step, _current_state, _predictions_series =
sess.run(
                [total_loss, train_step, currentState, predictions_series],
                feed_dict={
                    batchXHolder:batchX,
                    batchYHolder:batchY,
                    initState:_current_state
                })

            loss_list.append(_total_loss)

            # fix the cost summary later
            tf.summary.scalar(name="totalloss", tensor=_total_loss)

            if batch_idx%100 == 0:
                print("Step",batch_idx, "Loss", _total_loss)
                plot(loss_list, _predictions_series, batchX, batchY)

plt.ioff()
plt.show()
```

Computational graph

The following is the image of computational graph:

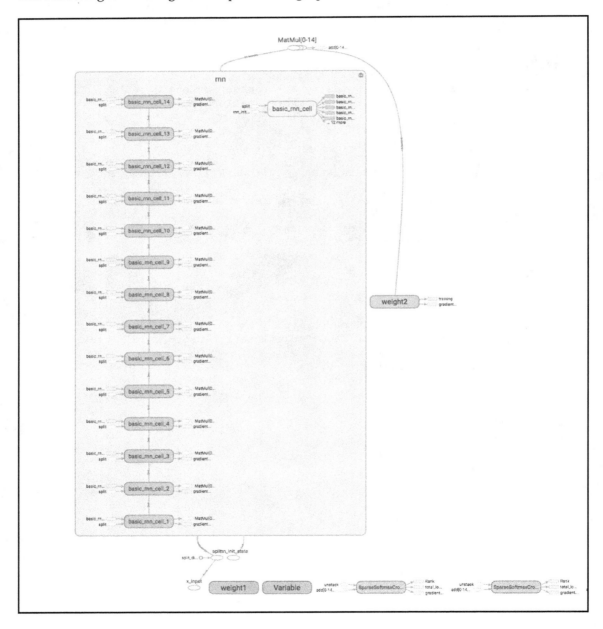

The output of the listing is shown as follows:

```
New data, epoch 0
Step 0 Loss 0.688437
Step 600 Loss 0.00107078
New data, epoch 1
Step 0 Loss 0.214923
Step 600 Loss 0.00111716
New data, epoch 2
Step 0 Loss 0.214962
Step 600 Loss 0.000730697
New data, epoch 3
Step 0 Loss 0.276177
Step 600 Loss 0.000362316
New data, epoch 4
Step 0 Loss 0.1641
Step 600 Loss 0.00025342
New data, epoch 5
Step 0 Loss 0.0947087
Step 600 Loss 0.000276762
```

Introduction to long short term memory networks

The vanishing gradient problem has appeared as the biggest obstacle to recurrent networks.

As the straight line changes along the x axis with a slight change in the y axis, the gradient shows change in all the weights with regard to change in error. If we don't know the gradient, we will not be able to adjust the weights in a direction that will reduce the loss or error, and our neural network ceases to learn.

Long short term memories (**LSTMs**) are designed to overcome the vanishing gradient problem. Retaining information for a larger duration of time is effectively their implicit behavior.

In standard RNNs, the repeating cell will have an elementary structure, such as a single **tanh** layer:

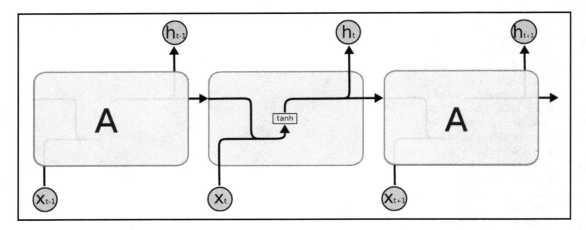

As seen in the preceding image, LSTMs also have a chain-like structure, but the recurrent cell has a different structure:

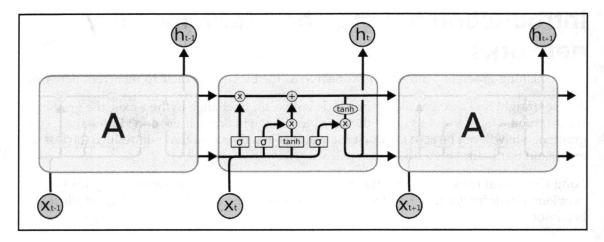

Life cycle of LSTM

The key to LSTMs is the cell state that is like a conveyor belt. It moves down the stream with minor linear interactions. It's straightforward for data to flow as unchanged:

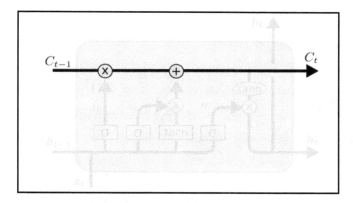

LSTM networks have the ability to either remove or add information to the cell state that is carefully regulated by structures known as gates.

1. The first step in an LSTM network is to determine what information we will be throwing away from the cell state. The decision is made by a sigmoid layer known as the **forget gate** layer. The layer looks at the previous state *h(t-1)* and current input *x(t)* and outputs a number between 0 and 1 for each number in the cell state *C(t–1)*, where 1 represents **absolutely keep this** while a 0 represents **entirely get rid of this**:

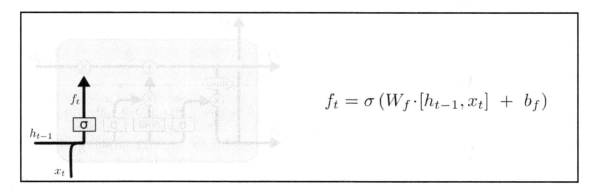

$$f_t = \sigma \left(W_f \cdot [h_{t-1}, x_t] + b_f \right)$$

2. The next step is to determine what new information we are going to persist in the cell state. Firstly, a sigmoid layer known as the input gate layer decides which values will be updated. Secondly, a *tanh* layer generates a vector of new candidate values C̃ that could be added to the state.

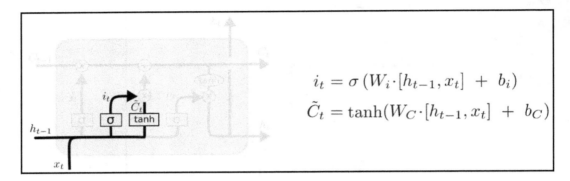

$$i_t = \sigma\left(W_i \cdot [h_{t-1}, x_t] + b_i\right)$$
$$\tilde{C}_t = \tanh(W_C \cdot [h_{t-1}, x_t] + b_C)$$

3. We will now update the old cell state *C(t−1)* to the new cell state *C(t)*. We multiply the old state by *f(t)*, forgetting the things we decided to forget earlier. Then we add *i(t)* ∗ C̃; these are the new candidate values scaled by the amount we decided to update each state value.

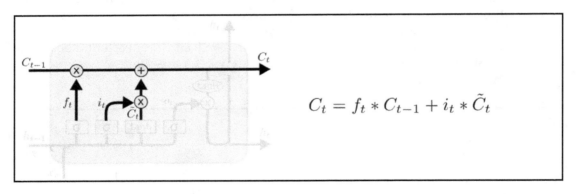

$$C_t = f_t * C_{t-1} + i_t * \tilde{C}_t$$

4. Finally, we decide on the output, which will be based on our cell state but will be a filtered or modified version. Firstly, we execute the sigmoid layer that determines what parts of the cell state we're going to output. Following which, we put the cell state through tanh to push the values to be between −1 and 1, and multiply it by the output of the sigmoid gate so that we only output the parts we decided to.

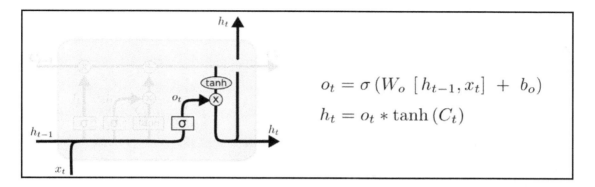

$$o_t = \sigma \left(W_o \left[h_{t-1}, x_t \right] + b_o \right)$$
$$h_t = o_t * \tanh \left(C_t \right)$$

LSTM implementation

LSTMs remember, forget, and pick what to pass on and then output depending on the current state and input. An LSTM has many more moving parts, but using the native TensorFlow API, it will be quite straightforward:

```
from __future__ import print_function, division
import tensorflow as tf
import numpy as np
import matplotlib.pyplot as plt
from tensorflow.contrib import rnn

"""
define all the constants
"""
numEpochs = 10
seriesLength = 50000
backpropagationLength = 15
stateSize = 4
numClasses = 2
echoStep = 3
batchSize = 5
num_batches = seriesLength // batchSize // backpropagationLength


"""
generate data
"""
def generateData():
    x = np.array(np.random.choice(2, seriesLength, p=[0.5, 0.5]))
    y = np.roll(x, echoStep)
    y[0:echoStep] = 0
```

```
        x = x.reshape((batchSize, -1))
        y = y.reshape((batchSize, -1))

        return (x, y)


"""
start computational graph
"""
batchXHolder = tf.placeholder(tf.float32, [batchSize,
backpropagationLength], name="x_input")
batchYHolder = tf.placeholder(tf.int32, [batchSize, backpropagationLength],
name="y_input")

# rnn replace
#initState = tf.placeholder(tf.float32, [batchSize, stateSize],
"rnn_init_state")

cellState = tf.placeholder(tf.float32, [batchSize, stateSize])
hiddenState = tf.placeholder(tf.float32, [batchSize, stateSize])
initState = rnn.LSTMStateTuple(cellState, hiddenState)

W = tf.Variable(np.random.rand(stateSize+1, stateSize), dtype=tf.float32,
name="weight1")
bias1 = tf.Variable(np.zeros((1,stateSize)), dtype=tf.float32)

W2 = tf.Variable(np.random.rand(stateSize, numClasses),dtype=tf.float32,
name="weight2")
bias2 = tf.Variable(np.zeros((1,numClasses)), dtype=tf.float32)

tf.summary.histogram(name="weights", values=W)


# Unpack columns
inputsSeries = tf.split(axis=1, num_or_size_splits=backpropagationLength,
value=batchXHolder)
labelsSeries = tf.unstack(batchYHolder, axis=1)

# Forward passes

# rnn replace
# cell = rnn.BasicRNNCell(stateSize)
# statesSeries, currentState = rnn.static_rnn(cell, inputsSeries,
initState)

cell = rnn.BasicLSTMCell(stateSize, state_is_tuple=True)
statesSeries, currentState = rnn.static_rnn(cell, inputsSeries, initState)
```

```
# calculate loss
logits_series = [tf.matmul(state, W2) + bias2 for state in statesSeries]
predictions_series = [tf.nn.softmax(logits) for logits in logits_series]

losses = [tf.nn.sparse_softmax_cross_entropy_with_logits(labels=labels,
logits=logits) for logits, labels in zip(logits_series,labelsSeries)]
total_loss = tf.reduce_mean(losses, name="total_loss")

train_step = tf.train.AdagradOptimizer(0.3).minimize(total_loss,
name="training")


"""
plot computation
"""
def plot(loss_list, predictions_series, batchX, batchY):
    plt.subplot(2, 3, 1)
    plt.cla()
    plt.plot(loss_list)

    for batchSeriesIdx in range(5):
        oneHotOutputSeries = np.array(predictions_series)[:,
batchSeriesIdx, :]
        singleOutputSeries = np.array([(1 if out[0] < 0.5 else 0) for out
in oneHotOutputSeries])

        plt.subplot(2, 3, batchSeriesIdx + 2)
        plt.cla()
        plt.axis([0, backpropagationLength, 0, 2])
        left_offset = range(backpropagationLength)
        plt.bar(left_offset, batchX[batchSeriesIdx, :], width=1,
color="blue")
        plt.bar(left_offset, batchY[batchSeriesIdx, :] * 0.5, width=1,
color="red")
        plt.bar(left_offset, singleOutputSeries * 0.3, width=1,
color="green")

    plt.draw()
    plt.pause(0.0001)


"""
run the graph
"""
with tf.Session() as sess:
    writer = tf.summary.FileWriter("logs", graph=tf.get_default_graph())
    sess.run(tf.global_variables_initializer())
    plt.ion()
```

```
        plt.figure()
        plt.show()
        loss_list = []

        for epoch_idx in range(numEpochs):
            x,y = generateData()

            # rnn remove
            # _current_state = np.zeros((batchSize, stateSize))

            _current_cell_state = np.zeros((batchSize, stateSize))
            _current_hidden_state = np.zeros((batchSize, stateSize))

            print("New data, epoch", epoch_idx)

            for batch_idx in range(num_batches):
                start_idx = batch_idx * backpropagationLength
                end_idx = start_idx + backpropagationLength

                batchX = x[:,start_idx:end_idx]
                batchY = y[:,start_idx:end_idx]

                _total_loss, _train_step, _current_state, _predictions_series =
        sess.run(
                    [total_loss, train_step, currentState, predictions_series],
                    feed_dict={
                        batchXHolder:batchX,
                        batchYHolder:batchY,
                        cellState: _current_cell_state,
                        hiddenState: _current_hidden_state
                    })

                _current_cell_state, _current_hidden_state = _current_state

                loss_list.append(_total_loss)

                # fix the cost summary later
                tf.summary.scalar(name="totalloss", tensor=_total_loss)

                if batch_idx%100 == 0:
                    print("Step",batch_idx, "Loss", _total_loss)
                    plot(loss_list, _predictions_series, batchX, batchY)

    plt.ioff()
    plt.show()
```

Computational graph

The following computational graph from TensorBoard describes the working of the LSTM network:

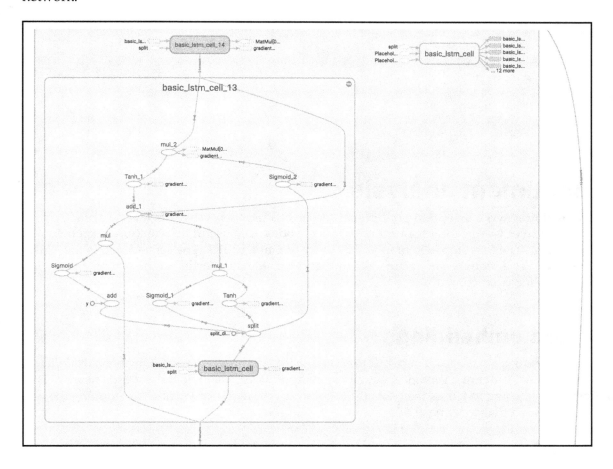

The output of the listing is shown as follows:

```
New data, epoch 0
Step 0 Loss 0.696803
Step 600 Loss 0.00743465
New data, epoch 1
Step 0 Loss 0.404039
Step 600 Loss 0.00243205
New data, epoch 2
Step 0 Loss 1.11536
Step 600 Loss 0.00140995
New data, epoch 3
Step 0 Loss 0.858743
Step 600 Loss 0.00141037
```

Sentiment analysis

We will now write an app to predict sentiments of a movie review. Reviews are made up of a sequence of words and the order of words encodes very useful information to predict sentiment. The first step is to map words to word embeddings. The second step is the RNN that receives a sequence of vectors as input and considers the order of the vectors to generate the prediction.

Word embeddings

We will now train a neural network for word to vector representation. Given a particular word in the center of a sentence, which is the input word, we look at the words nearby. The network is going to tell us the probability for every word in our vocabulary of being the nearby word that we choose.

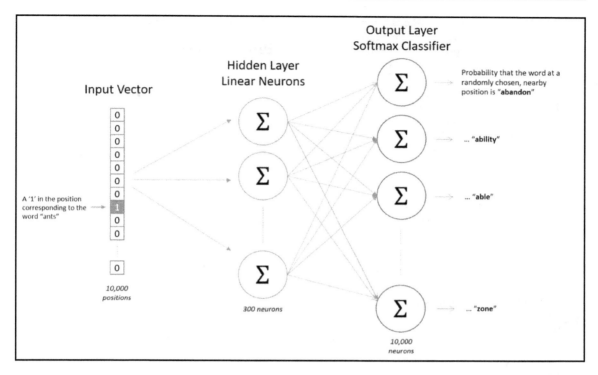

```
import time
import tensorflow as tf
import numpy as np
import utility
from tqdm import tqdm
from urllib.request import urlretrieve
from os.path import isfile, isdir
import zipfile
from collections import Counter
import random

dataDir = 'data'
dataFile = 'text8.zip'
datasetName = 'text 8 data set'

'''
track progress of file download
'''


class DownloadProgress(tqdm):
    lastBlock = 0
```

```
    def hook(self, blockNum=1, blockSize=1, totalSize=None):
        self.total = totalSize
        self.update((blockNum - self.lastBlock) * blockSize)
        self.lastBlock = blockNum


if not isfile(dataFile):
    with DownloadProgress(unit='B', unit_scale=True, miniters=1,
desc=datasetName) as progressBar:
        urlretrieve('http://mattmahoney.net/dc/text8.zip', dataFile,
progressBar.hook)

if not isdir(dataDir):
    with zipfile.ZipFile(dataFile) as zipRef:
        zipRef.extractall(dataDir)

with open('data/text8') as f:
    text = f.read()

'''
pre process the downloaded wiki text
'''
words = utility.preProcess(text)
print(words[:30])

print('Total words: {}'.format(len(words)))
print('Unique words: {}'.format(len(set(words))))


'''
convert words to integers
'''
int2vocab, vocab2int = utility.lookupTable(words)
intWords = [vocab2int[word] for word in words]
print('test')


'''
sub sampling (***think of words as int's***)
'''
threshold = 1e-5
wordCounts = Counter(intWords)
totalCount = len(intWords)
frequency = {word: count / totalCount for word, count in
wordCounts.items()}
probOfWords = {word: 1 - np.sqrt(threshold / frequency[word]) for word in
wordCounts}
trainWords = [word for word in intWords if random.random() < (1 -
probOfWords[word])]
```

```
'''
get window batches
'''


def getTarget(words, index, windowSize=5):
    rNum = np.random.randint(1, windowSize + 1)
    start = index - rNum if (index - rNum) > 0 else 0
    stop = index + rNum
    targetWords = set(words[start:index] + words[index + 1:stop + 1])

    return list(targetWords)


'''
Create a generator of word batches as a tuple (inputs, targets)
'''


def getBatches(words, batchSize, windowSize=5):
    nBatches = len(words) // batchSize
    print('no. of batches {}'.format(nBatches))

    # only full batches
    words = words[:nBatches * batchSize]

    start = 0
    for index in range(0, len(words), batchSize):
        x = []
        y = []
        stop = start + batchSize
        batchWords = words[start:stop]
        for idx in range(0, len(batchWords), 1):
            yBatch = getTarget(batchWords, idx, windowSize)
            y.extend(yBatch)
            x.extend([batchWords[idx]] * len(yBatch))
        start = stop + 1
        yield x, y


'''
start computational graph
'''
train_graph = tf.Graph()
with train_graph.as_default():
    netInputs = tf.placeholder(tf.int32, [None], name='inputS')
    netLabels = tf.placeholder(tf.int32, [None, None], name='labelS')
```

```
'''
create embedding layer
'''
nVocab = len(int2vocab)
nEmbedding = 300
with train_graph.as_default():
    embedding = tf.Variable(tf.random_uniform((nVocab, nEmbedding), -1, 1))
    embed = tf.nn.embedding_lookup(embedding, netInputs)


'''
Below, create weights and biases for the softmax layer. Then, use
tf.nn.sampled_softmax_loss to calculate the loss
'''
n_sampled = 100
with train_graph.as_default():
    soft_W = tf.Variable(tf.truncated_normal((nVocab, nEmbedding)))
    soft_b = tf.Variable(tf.zeros(nVocab), name="softmax_bias")

    # Calculate the loss using negative sampling
    loss = tf.nn.sampled_softmax_loss(
        weights=soft_W,
        biases=soft_b,
        labels=netLabels,
        inputs=embed,
        num_sampled=n_sampled,
        num_classes=nVocab)

    cost = tf.reduce_mean(loss)
    optimizer = tf.train.AdamOptimizer().minimize(cost)

'''
Here we're going to choose a few common words and few uncommon words. Then,
we'll print out the closest words to them.
It's a nice way to check that our embedding table is grouping together
words with similar semantic meanings.
'''
with train_graph.as_default():
    validSize = 16
    validWindow = 100

    validExamples = np.array(random.sample(range(validWindow), validSize //
2))
    validExamples = np.append(validExamples,
                              random.sample(range(1000, 1000 +
validWindow), validSize // 2))

    validDataset = tf.constant(validExamples, dtype=tf.int32)
```

```
    norm = tf.sqrt(tf.reduce_sum(tf.square(embedding), 1, keep_dims=True))
    normalizedEmbedding = embedding / norm
    valid_embedding = tf.nn.embedding_lookup(normalizedEmbedding,
validDataset)
    similarity = tf.matmul(valid_embedding,
tf.transpose(normalizedEmbedding))


'''
Train the network. Every 100 batches it reports the training loss. Every
1000 batches, it'll print out the validation
words.
'''
epochs = 10
batch_size = 1000
window_size = 10

with train_graph.as_default():
    saver = tf.train.Saver()

with tf.Session(graph=train_graph) as sess:
    iteration = 1
    loss = 0
    sess.run(tf.global_variables_initializer())

    for e in range(1, epochs + 1):
        batches = getBatches(trainWords, batch_size, window_size)
        start = time.time()
        for x, y in batches:

            feed = {netInputs: x,
                    netLabels: np.array(y)[:, None]}
            trainLoss, _ = sess.run([cost, optimizer], feed_dict=feed)

            loss += trainLoss

            if iteration % 100 == 0:
                end = time.time()
                print("Epoch {}/{}".format(e, epochs),
                      "Iteration: {}".format(iteration),
                      "Avg. Training loss: {:.4f}".format(loss / 100),
                      "{:.4f} sec/batch".format((end - start) / 100))
                loss = 0
                start = time.time()

            if iteration % 1000 == 0:
                sim = similarity.eval()
                for i in range(validSize):
```

```
                        validWord = int2vocab[validExamples[i]]
                        topK = 8
                        nearest = (-sim[i, :]).argsort()[1:topK + 1]
                        log = 'Nearest to %s:' % validWord
                        for k in range(topK):
                            closeWord = int2vocab[nearest[k]]
                            logStatement = '%s %s,' % (log, closeWord)
                        print(logStatement)

                iteration += 1
        save_path = saver.save(sess, "checkpoints/text8.ckpt")
        embed_mat = sess.run(normalizedEmbedding)


'''
Restore the trained network if you need to
'''
with train_graph.as_default():
    saver = tf.train.Saver()

with tf.Session(graph=train_graph) as sess:
    saver.restore(sess, tf.train.latest_checkpoint('checkpoints'))
    embed_mat = sess.run(embedding)


'''
Below we'll use T-SNE to visualize how our high-dimensional word vectors
cluster together. T-SNE is used to project
these vectors into two dimensions while preserving local structure.
'''
import matplotlib.pyplot as plt
from sklearn.manifold import TSNE
vizWords = 500
tsne = TSNE()
embedTSNE = tsne.fit_transform(embed_mat[:vizWords, :])

fig, ax = plt.subplots(figsize=(14, 14))
for idx in range(vizWords):
    plt.scatter(*embedTSNE[idx, :], color='steelblue')
    plt.annotate(int2vocab[idx], (embedTSNE[idx, 0], embedTSNE[idx, 1]),
alpha=0.7)
```

The output of the listing is as follows:

```
Total words: 16680599
 Unique words: 63641
 no. of batches 4626
Epoch 1/10 Iteration: 100 Avg. Training loss: 21.7284 0.3363 sec/batch
```

```
Epoch 1/10 Iteration: 1000 Avg. Training loss: 20.2269 0.3668 sec/batch

Nearest to but: universities, hungry, kyu, grandiose, edema, patty, stores,
psychometrics,
 Nearest to three: sulla, monuc, conjuring, ontological, auf, grimoire,
unpredictably, frenetic,

Nearest to world: turkle, spectroscopic, jules, servicio, sportswriter,
kamikazes, act, earns,
Epoch 1/10 Iteration: 1100 Avg. Training loss: 20.1983 0.3650 sec/batch
 Epoch 1/10 Iteration: 2000 Avg. Training loss: 19.1581 0.3767 sec/batch

Nearest to but: universities, hungry, edema, kyu, grandiose, stores, patty,
psychometrics,
 Nearest to three: monuc, sulla, unpredictably, grimoire, hickey,
ontological, conjuring, rays,
 Nearest to world: turkle, spectroscopic, jules, sportswriter, kamikazes,
alfons, servicio, act,
 ......
```

Sentiment analysis with an RNN

The following example shows the implementation of sentiment analysis using an RNN. It has fixed-length movie reviews encoded as integer values, which are then converted to word embedding (embedding vectors) passed to LSTM layers in a recurrent manner that pick the last prediction as the output sentiment:

```python
import numpy as np
import tensorflow as tf
from string import punctuation
from collections import Counter


'''
movie review dataset for sentiment analysis
'''
with open('data/reviews.txt', 'r') as f:
    movieReviews = f.read()
with open('data/labels.txt', 'r') as f:
    labels = f.read()


'''
data cleansing - remove punctuations
'''
text = ''.join([c for c in movieReviews if c not in punctuation])
```

```
movieReviews = text.split('\n')

text = ' '.join(movieReviews)
words = text.split()

print(text[:500])
print(words[:100])


'''
build a dictionary that maps words to integers
'''
counts = Counter(words)
vocabulary = sorted(counts, key=counts.get, reverse=True)
vocab2int = {word: i for i, word in enumerate(vocabulary, 1)}

reviewsInts = []
for review in movieReviews:
    reviewsInts.append([vocab2int[word] for word in review.split()])


'''
convert labels from positive and negative to 1 and 0 respectively
'''
labels = labels.split('\n')
labels = np.array([1 if label == 'positive' else 0 for label in labels])

reviewLengths = Counter([len(x) for x in reviewsInts])
print("Min review length are: {}".format(reviewLengths[0]))
print("Maximum review length are: {}".format(max(reviewLengths)))


'''
remove the review with zero length from the reviewsInts list
'''
nonZeroIndex = [i for i, review in enumerate(reviewsInts) if len(review) !=
0]
print(len(nonZeroIndex))


'''
turns out its the final review that has zero length. But that might not
always be the case, so let's make it more
general.
'''
reviewsInts = [reviewsInts[i] for i in nonZeroIndex]
labels = np.array([labels[i] for i in nonZeroIndex])
```

```
'''
create an array features that contains the data we'll pass to the network.
The data should come from reviewInts, since
we want to feed integers to the network. Each row should be 200 elements
long. For reviews shorter than 200 words,
left pad with 0s. That is, if the review is ['best', 'movie', 'renaira'],
[100, 40, 20] as integers, the row will look
like [0, 0, 0, ..., 0, 100, 40, 20]. For reviews longer than 200, use on
the first 200 words as the feature vector.
'''
seqLen = 200
features = np.zeros((len(reviewsInts), seqLen), dtype=int)
for i, row in enumerate(reviewsInts):
    features[i, -len(row):] = np.array(row)[:seqLen]

print(features[:10,:100])


'''
lets create training, validation and test data sets. trainX and trainY for
example.
also define a split percentage function 'splitPerc' as the percentage of
data to keep in the training
set. usually this is 0.8 or 0.9.
'''
splitPrec = 0.8
splitIndex = int(len(features)*0.8)
trainX, valX = features[:splitIndex], features[splitIndex:]
trainY, valY = labels[:splitIndex], labels[splitIndex:]

testIndex = int(len(valX)*0.5)
valX, testX = valX[:testIndex], valX[testIndex:]
valY, testY = valY[:testIndex], valY[testIndex:]

print("Train set: {}".format(trainX.shape), "\nValidation set:
{}".format(valX.shape), "\nTest set: {}".format(testX.shape))
print("label set: {}".format(trainY.shape), "\nValidation label set:
{}".format(valY.shape), "\nTest label set: {}".format(testY.shape))


'''
tensor-flow computational graph
'''
lstmSize = 256
lstmLayers = 1
batchSize = 500
learningRate = 0.001
```

```
nWords = len(vocab2int) + 1

# create graph object and add nodes to the graph
graph = tf.Graph()

with graph.as_default():
    inputData = tf.placeholder(tf.int32, [None, None], name='inputData')
    labels = tf.placeholder(tf.int32, [None, None], name='labels')
    keepProb = tf.placeholder(tf.float32, name='keepProb')


'''
let us create the embedding layer (word2vec)
'''
# number of neurons in hidden or embedding layer
embedSize = 300

with graph.as_default():
    embedding = tf.Variable(tf.random_uniform((nWords, embedSize), -1, 1))
    embed = tf.nn.embedding_lookup(embedding, inputData)


'''
lets use tf.contrib.rnn.BasicLSTMCell to create an LSTM cell, later add
drop out to it with
tf.contrib.rnn.DropoutWrapper. and finally create multiple LSTM layers with
tf.contrib.rnn.MultiRNNCell.
'''
with graph.as_default():
    with tf.name_scope("RNNLayers"):
        def createLSTMCell():
            lstm = tf.contrib.rnn.BasicLSTMCell(lstmSize,
reuse=tf.get_variable_scope().reuse)
            return tf.contrib.rnn.DropoutWrapper(lstm,
output_keep_prob=keepProb)

        cell = tf.contrib.rnn.MultiRNNCell([createLSTMCell() for _ in
range(lstmLayers)])

        initialState = cell.zero_state(batchSize, tf.float32)


'''
set tf.nn.dynamic_rnn to add the forward pass through the RNN. here we're
actually passing in vectors from the
embedding layer 'embed'.
'''
with graph.as_default():
```

```
    outputs, finalState = tf.nn.dynamic_rnn(cell, embed,
initial_state=initialState)


'''
final output will carry the sentiment prediction, therefore lets get the
last output with outputs[:, -1],
the we calculate the cost from that and labels.
'''
with graph.as_default():
    predictions = tf.contrib.layers.fully_connected(outputs[:, -1], 1,
activation_fn=tf.sigmoid)
    cost = tf.losses.mean_squared_error(labels, predictions)

    optimizer = tf.train.AdamOptimizer(learningRate).minimize(cost)


'''
now we can add a few nodes to calculate the accuracy which we'll use in the
validation pass.
'''
with graph.as_default():
    correctPred = tf.equal(tf.cast(tf.round(predictions), tf.int32),
labels)
    accuracy = tf.reduce_mean(tf.cast(correctPred, tf.float32))

'''
get batches
'''
def getBatches(x, y, batchSize=100):
    nBatches = len(x) // batchSize
    x, y = x[:nBatches * batchSize], y[:nBatches * batchSize]
    for i in range(0, len(x), batchSize):
        yield x[i:i + batchSize], y[i:i + batchSize]


'''
training phase
'''
epochs = 1

with graph.as_default():
    saver = tf.train.Saver()

with tf.Session(graph=graph) as sess:
    writer = tf.summary.FileWriter("logs", graph=tf.get_default_graph())
    sess.run(tf.global_variables_initializer())
    iteration = 1
    for e in range(epochs):
```

```
        state = sess.run(initialState)

        for i, (x, y) in enumerate(getBatches(trainX, trainY, batchSize),
1):
            feed = {inputData: x, labels: y[:, None], keepProb: 0.5,
initialState: state}

            loss, state, _ = sess.run([cost, finalState, optimizer],
feed_dict=feed)

            if iteration % 5 == 0:
                print("Epoch are: {}/{}".format(e, epochs), "Iteration is:
{}".format(iteration), "Train loss is: {:.3f}".format(loss))

            if iteration % 25 == 0:
                valAcc = []
                valState = sess.run(cell.zero_state(batchSize, tf.float32))
                for x, y in getBatches(valX, valY, batchSize):
                    feed = {inputData: x, labels: y[:, None], keepProb: 1,
initialState: valState}
                    batchAcc, valState = sess.run([accuracy, finalState],
feed_dict=feed)
                    valAcc.append(batchAcc)
                print("Val acc: {:.3f}".format(np.mean(valAcc)))
            iteration += 1
            saver.save(sess, "checkpoints/sentimentanalysis.ckpt")
    saver.save(sess, "checkpoints/sentimentanalysis.ckpt")

'''
testing phase
'''
testAcc = []
with tf.Session(graph=graph) as sess:
    saver.restore(sess, "checkpoints/sentiment.ckpt")

    testState = sess.run(cell.zero_state(batchSize, tf.float32))
    for i, (x, y) in enumerate(getBatches(testY, testY, batchSize), 1):
        feed = {inputData: x,
                labels: y[:, None],
                keepProb: 1,
                initialState: testState}
        batchAcc, testState = sess.run([accuracy, finalState],
feed_dict=feed)
        testAcc.append(batchAcc)
    print("Test accuracy is: {:.3f}".format(np.mean(testAcc)))
```

Computational graph

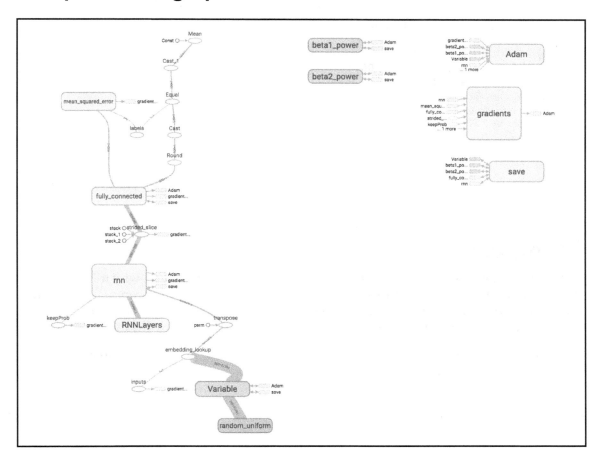

The output of the listing is shown as follows:

```
Train set: (20000, 200)
 Validation set: (2500, 200)
 Test set: (2500, 200)
 label set: (20000,)
 Validation label set: (2500,)
 Test label set: (2500,)
Val acc: 0.682
 Val acc: 0.692
 Val acc: 0.714
 Val acc: 0.808
 Val acc: 0.763
 Val acc: 0.826
 Val acc: 0.854
 Val acc: 0.872
```

Summary

In this chapter, you learned the basics of recurrent neural networks and why it is a useful mechanism for time series data processing. You learned about basic concepts such as states, word embeddings, and long-term memories. This was followed by an example to develop sentiment analysis system. We also implement recurrent neural networks using tensorflow.

In the next chapter, we look at a different kind of neural network called a **Generative Model**.

6
Generative Models

Generative models are the family of machine learning models that are used to describe how data is generated. To train a generative model we first accumulate a vast amount of data in any domain and later train a model to create or generate data like it.

In other words, these are the models that can learn to create data that is similar to data that we give them. One such approach is using **Generative Adversarial Networks (GANs)**, which will be discussed as part of this chapter in detail.

The following topics will be covered in this chapter:

- Introduction to generative models
- GANs

Generative models

There are two kinds of machine learning models: generative models and discriminative models. Let's examine the following list of classifiers: decision trees, neural networks, random forests, generalized boosted models, logistic regression, naive bayes, and **Support Vector Machine** (**SVM**). Most of these are classifiers and ensemble models. The odd one out here is Naive Bayes. It's the only generative model in the list. The others are examples of discriminative models.

The fundamental difference between generative and discriminative models lies in the underlying probability inference structure. In this chapter, we will study the key concepts of generative models like types and GANs, but before that, let's go through some of the key differences between generative and discriminative models.

Discriminative versus generative models

Discriminative models learn $P(Y|X)$, which is the conditional relationship between the target variable Y and features X. This is how least squares regression works, and it is the kind of inference pattern that gets used. It is an approach to sort out the relationship among variables.

Generative models aim for a complete probabilistic description of the dataset. With generative models, the goal is to develop the joint probability distribution $P(X, Y)$, either directly or by computing $P(Y | X)$ and $P(X)$ and then inferring the conditional probabilities required to classify newer data. This method requires more solid probabilistic thought than regression demands, but it provides a complete model of the probabilistic structure of the data. Knowing the joint distribution enables you to generate the data; hence, Naive Bayes is a generative model.

Suppose we have a supervised learning task, where x_i is the given features of the data points and y_i is the corresponding labels. One way to predict y on future x is to learn a function $f()$ from (x_i, y_i) that takes in x and outputs the most likely y. Such models fall in the category of discriminative models, as you are learning how to discriminate between x's from different classes. Methods like SVMs and neural networks fall into this category. Even if you're able to classify the data very accurately, you have no notion of how the data might have been generated.

The second approach is to model how the data might have been generated and learn a function $f(x,y)$ that gives a score to the configuration determined by x and y together. Then you can predict y for a new x by finding the y for which the score $f(x,y)$ is maximum. A canonical example of this is Gaussian mixture models.

Another example of this is: you can imagine x to be an image and y to be a kind of object like a dog, namely in the image. The probability written as $p(y|x)$ tells us how much the model believes that there is a dog, given an input image compared to all possibilities it knows about. Algorithms that try to model this probability map directly are called **discriminative models**.

Generative models, on the other hand, try to learn a function called the joint probability $p(y, x)$. We can read this as how much the model believes that x is an image and there is a dog y in it at the same time. These two probabilities are related and that could be written as $p(y, x) = p(x) p(y|x)$, with $p(x)$ being how likely it is that the input x is an image. The $p(x)$ probability is usually called a **density function** in literature.

The main reason to call these models generative ultimately connects to the fact that the model has access to the probability of both input and output at the same time. Using this, we can generate images of animals by sampling animal kinds y and new images x from $p(y, x)$.

We can mainly learn the density function $p(x)$ which only depends on the input space.

Both models are useful; however, comparatively, generative models have an interesting advantage over discriminative models, namely, they have the potential to understand and explain the underlying structure of the input data even when there are no labels available. This is very desirable when working in the real world.

Types of generative models

Discriminative models have been at the forefront of the recent success in the field of machine learning. Models make predictions that depend on a given input, although they are not able to generate new samples or data.

The idea behind the recent progress of generative modeling is to convert the generation problem to a prediction one and use deep learning algorithms to learn such a problem.

Autoencoders

One way to convert a generative to a discriminative problem can be by learning the mapping from the input space itself. For example, we want to learn an identity map that, for each image x, would ideally predict the same image, namely, $x = f(x)$, where f is the predictive model.

This model may not be of use in its current form, but from this, we can create a generative model.

Here, we create a model formed of two main components: an encoder model $q(h|x)$ that maps the input to another space, which is referred to as hidden or the latent space represented by h, and a decoder model $q(x|h)$ that learns the opposite mapping from the hidden input space.

These components--encoder and decoder--are connected together to create an end-to-end trainable model. Both the encoder and decoder models are neural networks of different architectures, for example, RNNs and Attention Nets, to get desired outcomes.

As the model is learned, we can remove the decoder from the encoder and then use them separately. To generate a new data sample, we can first generate a sample from the latent space and then feed that to the decoder to create a new sample from the output space.

Autoencoders are covered in more detail in Chapter 8, *Autoencoders* .

GAN

As seen with autoencoders, we can think of a general concept to create networks that will work together in a relationship, and training them will help us learn the latent spaces that allow us to generate new data samples.

Another type of generative network is GAN, where we have a generator model $q(x|h)$ to map the small dimensional latent space of h (which is usually represented as noise samples from a simple distribution) to the input space of x. This is quite similar to the role of decoders in autoencoders.

The deal is now to introduce a discriminative model $p(y|x)$, which tries to associate an input instance x to a yes/no binary answer y, about whether the generator model generated the input or was a genuine sample from the dataset we were training on.

Let's use the image example done previously. Assume that the generator model creates a new image, and we also have the real image from our actual dataset. If the generator model was right, the discriminator model would not be able to distinguish between the two images easily. If the generator model was poor, it would be very simple to tell which one was a fake or fraud and which one was real.

When both these models are coupled, we can train them end to end by assuring that the generator model is getting better over time to fool the discriminator model, while the discriminator model is trained to work on the harder problem of detecting frauds. Finally, we desire a generator model with outputs that are indistinguishable from the real data that we used for the training.

Through the initial parts of the training, the discriminator model can easily detect the samples coming from the actual dataset versus the ones generated synthetically by the generator model, which is just beginning to learn. As the generator gets better at modeling the dataset, we begin to see more and more generated samples that look similar to the dataset. The following example depicts the generated images of a GAN model learning over time:

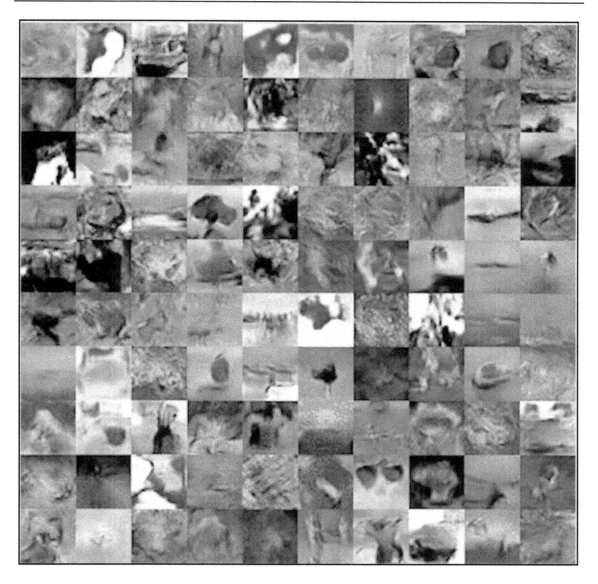

In the upcoming sections, we will discuss GANs in detail.

Sequence models

If the data is temporal in nature, then we can use specialized algorithms called **Sequence Models**. These models can learn the probability of the form $p(y|x\_n, x\_1)$, where i is an index signifying the location in the sequence and x_i is the ith input sample.

As an example, we can consider each word as a series of characters, each sentence as a series of words, and each paragraph as a series of sentences. Output y could be the sentiment of the sentence.

Using a similar trick from autoencoders, we can replace y with the next item in the series or sequence, namely $y = x\_n + 1$, allowing the model to learn.

GANs

GANs were introduced by a group of researchers at the University of Montreal led by *Ian Goodfellow*. The core idea behind a GAN model is to have two competing neural network models. One network takes the noise as input and generates samples (hence known as **generator**). The second model (known as **discriminator**) gets samples from both the generator and the actual training data, and should be able to differentiate between the two sources. Generative and discriminative networks are playing a continuous game, where the generator model is learning to generate more realistic samples or examples, and the discriminator is learning to get better and better at differentiating generated data from the real data. The two networks are trained simultaneously, and the goal is that the competition will make the generated samples indistinguishable from the real data:

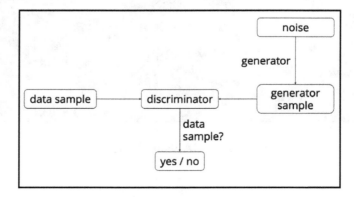

The analogy used to describe GANs is that the generator is like a forger that is attempting to produce some forged material, and the discriminator model is the police trying to detect the forged items. This may seem somewhat similar to reinforcement learning where the generator is getting a reward from the discriminator, allowing it to know whether the generated data is accurate or not. The key distinction with GANs is that we can backpropagate gradient information from the discriminator network back to the generator network, such that the generator knows how to adapt its parameters in order to generate output data that can fool the discriminator.

As of today, GANs have been mainly applied to model natural images. They provide best results in image generation tasks and also in generating images that are sharper than the ones trained using other generative methods based on maximum likelihood training objectives.

Here are some examples of images generated by GANs:

GAN with an example

For a deeper understanding of how GANs work, we'll use a GAN to solve a simple problem in TensorFlow, namely, learning to approximate a one-dimensional Gaussian distribution.

First, we will create the actual data distribution, a simple Gaussian with a mean of four and standard deviation of 0.5. It has a sample function that returns a given number of samples (sorted by value) from the distribution. The data distribution that we learn will look like the following diagram:

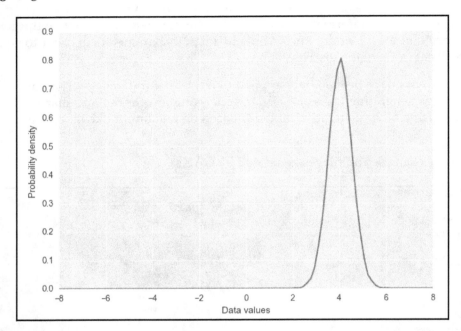

Generator input noise distribution is also defined with a similar sample function used for actual data.

Both generator and discriminator networks are very simple. Generator is a linear transformation passed through a non linearity (`softplus` function), followed by another linear transformation.

We kept the discriminator stronger than the generator; otherwise, it would not have enough capacity to learn to be able to differentiate accurately between generated and real samples. Hence, we made it a deeper neural network with a higher number of dimensions. We use *tanh* non linearities in all layers except the final one, which is a sigmoid (the output of which can be described as a probability).

We connect these networks as part of the TensorFlow graph and define loss functions for each of the networks so that the generator network will be simply fooling the discriminator network. The Gradient Descent Optimizer from TensorFlow with exponential learning rate decay is used as an optimizer.

To train the model, we draw samples from the data distribution and the noise distribution, and alternate between optimizing the parameters of the discriminator and the generator.

We will see that, at the start of the training method, the generator was generating a very different distribution to the real data. The network slowly learns to approximate it quite closely before converging to a narrower distribution focused on the mean of the input distribution. After training the networks, the two distributions look something like this:

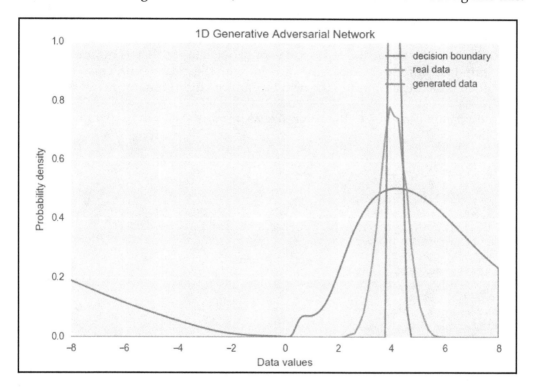

The problem of the generator network falling to a param setting where it generates a very narrow distribution or pattern of points is one of the major failures of GANs. The solution will be to allow the discriminator to look at multiple samples at once, a technique that we call minibatch discrimination. Minibatch discrimination is a method wherein the discriminator can glance at an entire batch of samples to determine whether they come from the generator network or from the actual data.

A summary of the method is as follows:

- Take the output of any intermediate layer of the discriminator network
- Multiply this output by a 3D tensor to generate a matrix of size *numOfKernels* * *kernelDim*
- Calculate the L1-distance between rows in this matrix across all samples in a batch, and then apply a negative exponential
- Minibatch features or properties for a sample are then the sum of these exponentiated distances
- Concatenate the actual input to the mini batch layer, that is, output of the previous or former discriminator layer with the created minibatch features, and then pass this as input to the next layer of the discriminator network

Minibatch discrimination makes the batch size as important as a hyperparameter:

```
import argparse
import numpy as np
import tensorflow as tf
import matplotlib.pyplot as plt
from matplotlib import animation
import seaborn as sns
from tensorflow.python.training.gradient_descent import
GradientDescentOptimizer

sns.set(color_codes=True)

seed = 42
np.random.seed(seed)
tf.set_random_seed(seed)


# gaussian data distribution
class DataDist(object):
    def __init__(self):
        self.mue = 4
        self.sigma = 0.5

    def sample(self, N):
        samples = np.random.normal(self.mue, self.sigma, N)
        samples.sort()
        return samples


# data distribution with noise
class GeneratorDist(object):
    def __init__(self, rnge):
```

```
        self.rnge = rnge

    def sample(self, N):
        return np.linspace(-self.rnge, self.rnge, N) + \
            np.random.random(N) * 0.01


# linear method
def linearUnit(input, output_dim, scope=None, stddev=1.0):
    with tf.variable_scope(scope or 'linearUnit'):
        weight = tf.get_variable(
            'weight',
            [input.get_shape()[1], output_dim],
            initializer=tf.random_normal_initializer(stddev=stddev)
        )
        bias = tf.get_variable(
            'bias',
            [output_dim],
            initializer=tf.constant_initializer(0.0)
        )
        return tf.matmul(input, weight) + bias


# generator network
def generatorNetwork(input, hidden_size):
    hidd0 = tf.nn.softplus(linearUnit(input, hidden_size, 'g0'))
    hidd1 = linearUnit(hidd0, 1, 'g1')
    return hidd1


# discriminator network
def discriminatorNetwork(input, h_dim, minibatch_layer=True):
    hidd0 = tf.nn.relu(linearUnit(input, h_dim * 2, 'd0'))
    hidd1 = tf.nn.relu(linearUnit(hidd0, h_dim * 2, 'd1'))

    if minibatch_layer:
        hidd2 = miniBatch(hidd1)
    else:
        hidd2 = tf.nn.relu(linearUnit(hidd1, h_dim * 2, scope='d2'))

    hidd3 = tf.sigmoid(linearUnit(hidd2, 1, scope='d3'))
    return hidd3


# minibatch
def miniBatch(input, numKernels=5, kernelDim=3):
    x = linearUnit(input, numKernels * kernelDim, scope='minibatch',
stddev=0.02)
```

```
        act = tf.reshape(x, (-1, numKernels, kernelDim))
        differences = tf.expand_dims(act, 3) - \
                tf.expand_dims(tf.transpose(act, [1, 2, 0]), 0)
        absDiffs = tf.reduce_sum(tf.abs(differences), 2)
        minibatchFeatures = tf.reduce_sum(tf.exp(-absDiffs), 2)
        return tf.concat([input, minibatchFeatures], 1)


# optimizer
def optimizer(loss, var_list):
    learning_rate = 0.001
    step = tf.Variable(0, trainable=False)
    optimizer = tf.train.AdamOptimizer(learning_rate).minimize(
        loss,
        global_step=step,
        var_list=var_list
    )
    return optimizer


# log
def log(x):
    return tf.log(tf.maximum(x, 1e-5))


class GAN(object):
    def __init__(self, params):
        with tf.variable_scope('Generator'):
            self.zee = tf.placeholder(tf.float32, shape=(params.batchSize,
1))
            self.Gee = generatorNetwork(self.zee, params.hidden_size)

        self.xVal = tf.placeholder(tf.float32, shape=(params.batchSize, 1))
        with tf.variable_scope('Discriminator'):
            self.Dis1 = discriminatorNetwork(
                self.xVal,
                params.hidden_size,
                params.minibatch
            )
        with tf.variable_scope('D', reuse=True):
            self.Dis2 = discriminatorNetwork(
                self.Gee,
                params.hidden_size,
                params.minibatch
            )

        self.lossD = tf.reduce_mean(-log(self.Dis1) - log(1 - self.Dis2))
        self.lossG = tf.reduce_mean(-log(self.Dis2))
```

```
        vars = tf.trainable_variables()
        self.dParams = [v for v in vars if v.name.startswith('D/')]
        self.gParams = [v for v in vars if v.name.startswith('G/')]

        self.optD = optimizer(self.lossD, self.dParams)
        self.optG = optimizer(self.lossG, self.gParams)


'''
Train GAN model
'''
def trainGan(model, data, gen, params):
    animFrames = []

    with tf.Session() as session:
        tf.local_variables_initializer().run()
        tf.global_variables_initializer().run()

        for step in range(params.numSteps + 1):
            x = data.sample(params.batchSize)
            z = gen.sample(params.batchSize)
            lossD, _, = session.run([model.lossD, model.optD], {
                model.x: np.reshape(x, (params.batchSize, 1)),
                model.z: np.reshape(z, (params.batchSize, 1))
            })

            z = gen.sample(params.batchSize)
            lossG, _ = session.run([model.lossG, model.optG], {
                model.z: np.reshape(z, (params.batchSize, 1))
            })

            if step % params.log_every == 0:
                print('{}: {:.4f}\t{:.4f}'.format(step, lossD, lossG))

            if params.animPath and (step % params.animEvery == 0):
                animFrames.append(
                    getSamples(model, session, data, gen.range,
params.batchSize)
                )

        if params.animPath:
            saveAnimation(animFrames, params.animPath, gen.range)
        else:
            samps = getSamples(model, session, data, gen.range,
params.batchSize)
            plotDistributions(samps, gen.range)
```

```
def getSamples(
        model,
        session,
        data,
        sampleRange,
        batchSize,
        numPoints=10000,
        numBins=100
):
    xs = np.linspace(-sampleRange, sampleRange, numPoints)
    binss = np.linspace(-sampleRange, sampleRange, numBins)

    # decision boundary
    db = np.zeros((numPoints, 1))
    for i in range(numPoints // batchSize):
        db[batchSize * i:batchSize * (i + 1)] = session.run(
            model.D1,
            {
                model.x: np.reshape(
                    xs[batchSize * i:batchSize * (i + 1)],
                    (batchSize, 1)
                )
            }
        )

    # data distribution
    d = data.sample(numPoints)
    pds, _ = np.histogram(d, bins=binss, density=True)

    zs = np.linspace(-sampleRange, sampleRange, numPoints)
    g = np.zeros((numPoints, 1))
    for i in range(numPoints // batchSize):
        g[batchSize * i:batchSize * (i + 1)] = session.run(
            model.G,
            {
                model.z: np.reshape(
                    zs[batchSize * i:batchSize * (i + 1)],
                    (batchSize, 1)
                )
            }
        )
    pgs, _ = np.histogram(g, bins=binss, density=True)

    return db, pds, pgs


def plotDistributions(samps, sampleRange):
    db, pd, pg = samps
```

```
        dbX = np.linspace(-sampleRange, sampleRange, len(db))
        pX = np.linspace(-sampleRange, sampleRange, len(pd))
        f, ax = plt.subplots(1)
        ax.plot(dbX, db, label='Decision Boundary')
        ax.set_ylim(0, 1)
        plt.plot(pX, pd, label='Real Data')
        plt.plot(pX, pg, label='Generated Data')
        plt.title('1D Generative Adversarial Network')
        plt.xlabel('Data Values')
        plt.ylabel('Probability Density')
        plt.legend()
        plt.show()


def saveAnimation(animFrames, animPath, sampleRange):
    f, ax = plt.subplots(figsize=(6, 4))
    f.suptitle('1D GAN', fontsize=15)
    plt.xlabel('dataValues')
    plt.ylabel('probabilityDensity')
    ax.set_xlim(-6, 6)
    ax.set_ylim(0, 1.4)
    lineDb, = ax.plot([], [], label='decision boundary')
    linePd, = ax.plot([], [], label='real data')
    linePg, = ax.plot([], [], label='generated data')
    frameNumber = ax.text(
        0.02,
        0.95,
        '',
        horizontalalignment='left',
        verticalalignment='top',
        transform=ax.transAxes
    )
    ax.legend()

    db, pd, _ = animFrames[0]
    dbX = np.linspace(-sampleRange, sampleRange, len(db))
    pX = np.linspace(-sampleRange, sampleRange, len(pd))

    def init():
        lineDb.set_data([], [])
        linePd.set_data([], [])
        linePg.set_data([], [])
        frameNumber.set_text('')
        return (lineDb, linePd, linePg, frameNumber)

    def animate(i):
        frameNumber.set_text(
            'Frame: {}/{}'.format(i, len(animFrames))
```

```
            )
            db, pd, pg = animFrames[i]
            lineDb.set_data(dbX, db)
            linePd.set_data(pX, pd)
            linePg.set_data(pX, pg)
            return (lineDb, linePd, linePg, frameNumber)

    anim = animation.FuncAnimation(
        f,
        animate,
        init_func=init,
        frames=len(animFrames),
        blit=True
    )
    anim.save(animPath, fps=30, extra_args=['-vcodec', 'libx264'])


# start gan modeling
def gan(args):
    model = GAN(args)
    trainGan(model, DataDist(), GeneratorDist(range=8), args)


# input arguments
def parseArguments():
    argParser = argparse.ArgumentParser()
    argParser.add_argument('--num-steps', type=int, default=5000,
                           help='the number of training steps to take')
    argParser.add_argument('--hidden-size', type=int, default=4,
                           help='MLP hidden size')
    argParser.add_argument('--batch-size', type=int, default=8,
                           help='the batch size')
    argParser.add_argument('--minibatch', action='store_true',
                           help='use minibatch discrimination')
    argParser.add_argument('--log-every', type=int, default=10,
                           help='print loss after this many steps')
    argParser.add_argument('--anim-path', type=str, default=None,
                           help='path to the output animation file')
    argParser.add_argument('--anim-every', type=int, default=1,
                           help='save every Nth frame for animation')
    return argParser.parse_args()


# start the gan app
if __name__ == '__main__':
    gan(parseArguments())
```

Output Listing:

```
 0:  6.6300  0.1449
 10:  6.5390  0.1655
 20:  6.4552  0.1866
 30:  6.3789  0.2106
 40:  6.3190  0.2372
 50:  6.2814  0.2645
 60:  6.2614  0.2884
 70:  6.2556  0.3036
 80:  6.2814  0.3104
 90:  6.2796  0.3113
100:  6.3008  0.3106
110:  6.2923  0.3112
120:  6.2792  0.3153
130:  6.3299  0.3196
140:  6.3512  0.3205
150:  6.2999  0.3197
160:  6.3513  0.3236
170:  6.3521  0.3291
180:  6.3377  0.3292
```

Types of GANs

The following section shows different types of GANs, for example, Vanilla GAN, Conditional GAN etc. Refer to https://arxiv.org for further information on the papers. The following description about each GAN network is taken from the respective paper on https://arxiv.org.

Vanilla GAN

Vanilla GANs has two networks called generator network and a discriminator network. Both the networks are trained at the same time and compete or battle against each other in a minimax play. Generator network is trained or prepared such that it can fool the discriminator network by creating the real images as per the input, and the discriminator is trained not to be fooled by the generator network.

 For further reading on Vanilla GAN refer to https://arxiv.org/abs/1406.2661.

Conditional GAN

GANs was started as a novel way of generative training models. These are GAN networks that utilize extra label data. It results in excellent quality images and being able to control to an extent how generated images will look. This model can be used to learn a multi-modal model.

For further reading on Conditional GAN refer to https://arxiv.org/abs/1411.1784.

Info GAN

GANs that can encode or learn important image features or disentangled representations in an unsupervised manner. An example is to encode the rotation of a digit. Info GANs also maximizes the mutual information between a small subset of the latent variables and the observation.

For further reading on Info GAN refer to https://arxiv.org/abs/1606.03657

Wasserstein GAN

WGAN is an option to regular GAN training. WGANs have loss functions that correlate with image quality. Additionally, the stability of the training improves and is not as dependent on the architecture and provide significant learning curves useful for debugging.

For further reading on Wasserstein GAN refer to https://arxiv.org/abs/1701.07875

Coupled GAN

Coupled GANs is used for generating sets of like images in two separate domains. It consists of set of GANs each accountable for generating images in the single domain. The Coupled GANs learns a joint distribution from images in the two domains which are drawn separately from the marginal distributions of the unique domains.

 For further reading on Coupled GAN refer to `https://arxiv.org/abs/`
`1606.07536`

Summary

Generative models are a fast advancing area of study and research. As we proceed to advance these models and grow the training and datasets, we can expect to generate data examples that depict completely believable images, finally. This can be used in several applications such as image denoising, painting, structured prediction, and exploration in reinforcement learning.

The deeper promise of this effort is that, in the process of building generative models, we will enrich the computer with an understanding of the world and what elements it is made up of.

7
Deep Belief Networking

A **deep belief network** (**DBN**) is a class of deep neural network, composed of multiple layers of hidden units, with connections between the layers; where a DBN differs is these hidden units don't interact with other units within each layer. A DBN can learn to probabilistically reconstruct its input without supervision, when trained, using a set of training datasets. It is a joint (multivariate) distributions over large numbers of random variables that interact with each other. These representations sit at the intersection of statistics and computer science, relying on concepts from probability theory, graph algorithms, machine learning, and more.

The layers act as feature detectors. After the training step, a DBN can be trained with supervision to perform classification.

We will be covering the following chapters in the chapter:

- Understanding deep belief networks
- Model training
- Predicting the label
- Finding the accuracy of the model
- DBN implementation for the MNIST dataset
- Effect of the number of neurons in an RBM Layer in a DBN
- DBNs with two RBM layers
- Classifying the NotMNIST dataset with a DBN

Understanding deep belief networks

DBNs can be considered a composition of simple, unsupervised networks such as **Restricted Boltzmann machines (RBMs)** or autoencoders; in these, each subnetwork's hidden layer serves as the visible layer for the next. An RBM is an undirected, generative model with an input layer (which is visible) and a hidden layer, with connections between the layers but not within layers. This topology leads to a fast, layer-by-layer, unsupervised training procedure. Contrastive divergence is applied to each subnetwork, starting from the lowest pair of layers (the lowest visible layer is a training set).

DBNs are trained (greedily), one layer at a time, which makes it one of the first effective deep learning algorithms. There are many implementations and uses of DBNs in real-life applications and scenarios; we will be looking at using a DBN to classify MNIST and NotMNIST datasets.

DBN implementation

This class instantiates the Restricted Boltzmann machines (RBN) layers and the cost functions. The **DeepBeliefNetwork** class is itself a subclass of the **Model**:

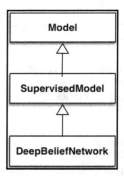

Class initialization

In DBN initialization, the `Model` class's initialization method `__init__(self, name)` is called. The `Model` class references the following:

- **Input data**: `self.input_data`
- **Input labels**: `self.input_labels`
- **Cost**: `self.cost`

- **Number of nodes in final layer**: `self.layer_nodes`
- **TensorFlow session**: `self.tf_session`
- **TensorFlow graph**: `self.tf_graph= tf.graph`

```
class Model(object):
    """Class representing an abstract Model."""

    def __init__(self, name):
        """Constructor.

        :param name: name of the model, used as filename.
            string, default 'dae'
        """
        self.name = name
        self.model_path = os.path.join(Config().models_dir, self.name)

        self.input_data = None
        self.input_labels = None
        self.keep_prob = None
        self.layer_nodes = []   # list of layers of the final network
        self.train_step = None
        self.cost = None

        # tensorflow objects
        self.tf_graph = tf.Graph()
        self.tf_session = None
        self.tf_saver = None
        self.tf_merged_summaries = None
        self.tf_summary_writer = None
```

Other variables that are defined are the loss functions, which should be one of the following:

```
["cross_entropy", "softmax_cross_entropy", "mse"]
```

Code Listing for **DeepBeliefNetwork** class is given below. The __init__() function is shown in the following code. Here all the variables, such as array of parameters for each RBM layer are specified. We are also making a call to the __init__() function of `SupervisedModel`, which is the super class for the `DeepBeliefNetwork` class.

Two important parameters to initialize are:

- `self.rbms = []`: Array of RBM class instances
- `self.rbm_graphs = []`: An array `tf.Graph` for each of those RBMs

```
class DeepBeliefNetwork(SupervisedModel):
    """Implementation of Deep Belief Network for Supervised Learning.

    The interface of the class is sklearn-like.
    """

    def __init__(
        self, rbm_layers, name='dbn', do_pretrain=False,
        rbm_num_epochs=[10], rbm_gibbs_k=[1],
        rbm_gauss_visible=False, rbm_stddev=0.1, rbm_batch_size=[10],
        rbm_learning_rate=[0.01], finetune_dropout=1,
        finetune_loss_func='softmax_cross_entropy',
        finetune_act_func=tf.nn.sigmoid, finetune_opt='sgd',
        finetune_learning_rate=0.001, finetune_num_epochs=10,
            finetune_batch_size=20, momentum=0.5):
        SupervisedModel.__init__(self, name)

        self.loss_func = finetune_loss_func
        self.learning_rate = finetune_learning_rate
        self.opt = finetune_opt
        self.num_epochs = finetune_num_epochs
        self.batch_size = finetune_batch_size
        self.momentum = momentum
        self.dropout = finetune_dropout

        self.loss = Loss(self.loss_func)
        self.trainer = Trainer(
            finetune_opt, learning_rate=finetune_learning_rate,
            momentum=momentum)

        self.do_pretrain = do_pretrain
        self.layers = rbm_layers
        self.finetune_act_func = finetune_act_func

        # Model parameters
        self.encoding_w_ = []  # list of matrices of encoding weights per
layer
        self.encoding_b_ = []  # list of arrays of encoding biases per
layer

        self.softmax_W = None
        self.softmax_b = None
```

```
        rbm_params = {
            'num_epochs': rbm_num_epochs, 'gibbs_k': rbm_gibbs_k,
            'batch_size': rbm_batch_size, 'learning_rate':
rbm_learning_rate}

        for p in rbm_params:
            if len(rbm_params[p]) != len(rbm_layers):
                # The current parameter is not specified by the user,
                # should default it for all the layers
                rbm_params[p] = [rbm_params[p][0] for _ in rbm_layers]

        self.rbms = []
        self.rbm_graphs = []

        for l, layer in enumerate(rbm_layers):
            rbm_str = 'rbm-' + str(l+1)

            if l == 0 and rbm_gauss_visible:
                self.rbms.append(
                    rbm.RBM(
                        name=self.name + '-' + rbm_str,
                        num_hidden=layer,
                        learning_rate=rbm_params['learning_rate'][l],
                        num_epochs=rbm_params['num_epochs'][l],
                        batch_size=rbm_params['batch_size'][l],
                        gibbs_sampling_steps=rbm_params['gibbs_k'][l],
                        visible_unit_type='gauss', stddev=rbm_stddev))

            else:
                self.rbms.append(
                    rbm.RBM(
                        name=self.name + '-' + rbm_str,
                        num_hidden=layer,
                        learning_rate=rbm_params['learning_rate'][l],
                        num_epochs=rbm_params['num_epochs'][l],
                        batch_size=rbm_params['batch_size'][l],
                        gibbs_sampling_steps=rbm_params['gibbs_k'][l]))

            self.rbm_graphs.append(tf.Graph())
```

Notice how RBM layers are constructed from the rbm_layers array:

```
for l, layer in enumerate(rbm_layers):
        rbm_str = 'rbm-' + str(l+1)

        if l == 0 and rbm_gauss_visible:
            self.rbms.append(
```

```
                       rbm.RBM(
                           name=self.name + '-' + rbm_str,
                           num_hidden=layer,
                           learning_rate=rbm_params['learning_rate'][l],
                           num_epochs=rbm_params['num_epochs'][l],
                           batch_size=rbm_params['batch_size'][l],
                           gibbs_sampling_steps=rbm_params['gibbs_k'][l],
                           visible_unit_type='gauss', stddev=rbm_stddev))
            else:
                self.rbms.append(
                    rbm.RBM(
                        name=self.name + '-' + rbm_str,
                        num_hidden=layer,
                        learning_rate=rbm_params['learning_rate'][l],
                        num_epochs=rbm_params['num_epochs'][l],
                        batch_size=rbm_params['batch_size'][l],
                        gibbs_sampling_steps=rbm_params['gibbs_k'][l]))
```

RBM class

For each RBM layer, an **RBM** class is initialized. This class extends the **UnsupervisedModel** and **Model** classes:

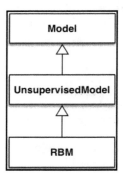

Details of the **RBM** class __init__(..) function are specified in the following code:

```
class RBM(UnsupervisedModel):
    """Restricted Boltzmann Machine implementation using TensorFlow.

    The interface of the class is sklearn-like.
    """

    def __init__(
        self, num_hidden, visible_unit_type='bin',
```

```
            name='rbm', loss_func='mse', learning_rate=0.01,
            regcoef=5e-4, regtype='none', gibbs_sampling_steps=1,
                batch_size=10, num_epochs=10, stddev=0.1):
            """Constructor.

            :param num_hidden: number of hidden units
            :param loss_function: type of loss function
            :param visible_unit_type: type of the visible units (bin or gauss)
            :param gibbs_sampling_steps: optional, default 1
            :param stddev: default 0.1. Ignored if visible_unit_type is not
'gauss'
            """
            UnsupervisedModel.__init__(self, name)

            self.loss_func = loss_func
            self.learning_rate = learning_rate
            self.num_epochs = num_epochs
            self.batch_size = batch_size
            self.regtype = regtype
            self.regcoef = regcoef

            self.loss = Loss(self.loss_func)

            self.num_hidden = num_hidden
            self.visible_unit_type = visible_unit_type
            self.gibbs_sampling_steps = gibbs_sampling_steps
            self.stddev = stddev

            self.W = None
            self.bh_ = None
            self.bv_ = None

            self.w_upd8 = None
            self.bh_upd8 = None
            self.bv_upd8 = None

            self.cost = None

            self.input_data = None
            self.hrand = None
            self.vrand = None
```

Once the `rbm` graphs are initialized they are appended to the the TensorFlow graph:

```
        self.rbm_graphs.append(tf.Graph())
```

Pretraining the DBN

In this section, we look at how a DBN is pretrained:

```
class RBM(UnsupervisedModel):
...
  def pretrain(self, train_set, validation_set=None):
    """Perform Unsupervised pretraining of the DBN."""
    self.do_pretrain = True

    def set_params_func(rbmmachine, rbmgraph):
    params = rbmmachine.get_parameters(graph=rbmgraph)
     self.encoding_w_.append(params['W'])
     self.encoding_b_.append(params['bh_'])

    return SupervisedModel.pretrain_procedure(
      self, self.rbms, self.rbm_graphs, set_params_func=set_params_func,
      train_set=train_set, validation_set=validation_set)
```

This in turn calls `SupervisedModel.pretrain_procedure(..)`, which takes the following parameters:

- `layer_objs`: A list of model objects (autoencoders or RBMs)
- `layer_graphs`: A list of model `tf.Graph` objects
- `set_params_func`: The function used to set the parameters after pretraining
- `train_set`: The training set
- `validation_set`: The validation set

This function returns data encoded by the last layer:

```
def pretrain_procedure(self, layer_objs, layer_graphs, set_params_func,
  train_set, validation_set=None):
  next_train = train_set
  next_valid = validation_set

  for l, layer_obj in enumerate(layer_objs):
    print('Training layer {}...'.format(l + 1))
    next_train, next_valid = self._pretrain_layer_and_gen_feed(
      layer_obj, set_params_func, next_train, next_valid,
      layer_graphs[l])

  return next_train, next_valid
```

This in turn calls `self._pretrain_layer_and_gen_feed(...)`:

```
def _pretrain_layer_and_gen_feed(self, layer_obj, set_params_func,
                                 train_set, validation_set, graph):
    layer_obj.fit(train_set, train_set,
                  validation_set, validation_set, graph=graph)

    with graph.as_default():
        set_params_func(layer_obj, graph)

        next_train = layer_obj.transform(train_set, graph=graph)
        if validation_set is not None:
            next_valid = layer_obj.transform(validation_set, graph=graph)
        else:
            next_valid = None

    return next_train, next_valid
```

Inside the preceding function, each `layer_obj` is called **iteratively**.

Model training

Model training is implemented in the `fit(..)` method. It takes the following parameters:

- `train_X`: `array_like, shape (n_samples, n_features)`, Training data
- `train_Y`: `array_like, shape (n_samples, n_classes)`, Training labels
- `val_X`: `array_like, shape (N, n_features) optional, (default = None)`, Validation data
- `val_Y`: `array_like, shape (N, n_classes) optional, (default = None)`, Validation labels
- `graph`: `tf.Graph, optional (default = None)`, TensorFlow Graph object

Next, we look at the implementation of `fit(...)` function where the model is trained and saved in the model path specified by `model_path`.

```
def fit(self, train_X, train_Y, val_X=None, val_Y=None, graph=None):

    if len(train_Y.shape) != 1:
        num_classes = train_Y.shape[1]
    else:
        raise Exception("Please convert the labels with one-hot encoding.")

    g = graph if graph is not None else self.tf_graph
```

```
with g.as_default():
    # Build model
    self.build_model(train_X.shape[1], num_classes)
    with tf.Session() as self.tf_session:
        # Initialize tf stuff
        summary_objs = tf_utils.init_tf_ops(self.tf_session)
        self.tf_merged_summaries = summary_objs[0]
        self.tf_summary_writer = summary_objs[1]
        self.tf_saver = summary_objs[2]
        # Train model
        self._train_model(train_X, train_Y, val_X, val_Y)
        # Save model
        self.tf_saver.save(self.tf_session, self.model_path)
```

Predicting the label

Prediction of the label can be made by calling the following method:

```
def predict(self, test_X):
    with self.tf_graph.as_default():
        with tf.Session() as self.tf_session:
            self.tf_saver.restore(self.tf_session, self.model_path)
            feed = {
                self.input_data: test_X,
                self.keep_prob: 1
            }
            return self.mod_y.eval(feed)
```

Finding the accuracy of the model

Accuracy of the model is found by computing mean accuracy over the test set. It is implemented in the following method:

```
def score(self, test_X, test_Y):
    ...
```

Here, the parameters are as follows:

- `test_X: array_like, shape (n_samples, n_features)`, Test data
- `test_Y: array_like, shape (n_samples, n_features)`, Test labels
- `return float`: mean accuracy over the test set

```
def score(self, test_X, test_Y):
    with self.tf_graph.as_default():
        with tf.Session() as self.tf_session:
            self.tf_saver.restore(self.tf_session, self.model_path)
            feed = {
                self.input_data: test_X,
                self.input_labels: test_Y,
                self.keep_prob: 1
            }
            return self.accuracy.eval(feed)
```

In the next section, we will look at how DBN implementation can be used on the MNIST dataset.

DBN implementation for the MNIST dataset

Let's look at how the DBN class implemented earlier is used for the MNIST dataset.

Loading the dataset

First, we load the dataset from `idx3` and `idx1` formats into test, train, and validation sets. We need to import TensorFlow common utilities that are defined in the common module explained here:

```
import tensorflow as tf
from common.models.boltzmann import dbn
from common.utils import datasets, utilities

trainX, trainY, validX, validY, testX, testY =
    datasets.load_mnist_dataset(mode='supervised')
```

You can find details about `load_mnist_dataset()` in the following code listing. As `mode='supervised'` is set, the train, test, and validation labels are returned:

```
def load_mnist_dataset(mode='supervised', one_hot=True):
    mnist = input_data.read_data_sets("MNIST_data/", one_hot=one_hot)
    # Training set
    trX = mnist.train.images
    trY = mnist.train.labels
    # Validation set
    vlX = mnist.validation.images
    vlY = mnist.validation.labels
    # Test set
    teX = mnist.test.images
```

```
teY = mnist.test.labels
if mode == 'supervised':
    return trX, trY, vlX, vlY, teX, teY
elif mode == 'unsupervised':
    return trX, vlX, teX
```

Input parameters for a DBN with 256-Neuron RBM layers

We will initialize various parameters that are needed by the DBN class defined earlier:

```
finetune_act_func = tf.nn.relu
rbm_layers = [256]
do_pretrain = True
name = 'dbn'
rbm_layers = [256]
finetune_act_func ='relu'
do_pretrain = True
rbm_learning_rate = [0.001]
rbm_num_epochs = [1]
rbm_gibbs_k= [1]
rbm_stddev= 0.1
rbm_gauss_visible= False
momentum= 0.5
rbm_batch_size= [32]
finetune_learning_rate = 0.01
finetune_num_epochs = 1
finetune_batch_size = 32
finetune_opt = 'momentum'
finetune_loss_func = 'softmax_cross_entropy'
finetune_dropout = 1
finetune_act_func = tf.nn.sigmoid
```

Once the parameters are defined, let's run the DBN network on the MNIST dataset:

```
srbm = dbn.DeepBeliefNetwork(
    name=name, do_pretrain=do_pretrain,
    rbm_layers=rbm_layers,
    finetune_act_func=finetune_act_func,
    rbm_learning_rate=rbm_learning_rate,
    rbm_num_epochs=rbm_num_epochs, rbm_gibbs_k = rbm_gibbs_k,
    rbm_gauss_visible=rbm_gauss_visible, rbm_stddev=rbm_stddev,
    momentum=momentum, rbm_batch_size=rbm_batch_size,
    finetune_learning_rate=finetune_learning_rate,
    finetune_num_epochs=finetune_num_epochs,
    finetune_batch_size=finetune_batch_size,
```

```
        finetune_opt=finetune_opt, finetune_loss_func=finetune_loss_func,
        finetune_dropout=finetune_dropout
        )

print(do_pretrain)
if do_pretrain:
    srbm.pretrain(trainX, validX)

# finetuning
print('Start deep belief net finetuning...')
srbm.fit(trainX, trainY, validX, validY)

# Test the model
print('Test set accuracy: {}'.format(srbm.score(testX, testY)))
```

Output for a DBN with 256-neuron RBN layers

The output of the preceding listing shows the test set's accuracy:

```
Reconstruction loss: 0.156712: 100%|███████████| 5/5 [00:49&lt;00:00,
9.99s/it]
Start deep belief net finetuning...
Tensorboard logs dir for this run is /home/ubuntu/.yadlt/logs/run53
Accuracy: 0.0868: 100%|███████████| 1/1 [00:04&lt;00:00, 4.09s/it]
Test set accuracy: 0.0868000015616
```

Overall accuracy and Test set accuracy is quite low. With the increase in number of iterations it improves. Let us run same sample with 20 epochs

```
Reconstruction loss: 0.120337: 100%|███████████| 20/20 [03:07<00:00,
8.79s/it]
Start deep belief net finetuning...
Tensorboard logs dir for this run is /home/ubuntu/.yadlt/logs/run80
Accuracy: 0.105: 100%|███████████| 1/1 [00:04<00:00, 4.16s/it]
Test set accuracy: 0.10339999944
```

As can be seen the reconstruction loss has come down and the Test set accuracy has improved by 20% to 0.10339999944

Let us increase the number of Epochs to 40. Output is shown below

```
Reconstruction loss: 0.104798: 100%|███████████| 40/40 [06:20<00:00,
9.18s/it]
Start deep belief net finetuning...
Tensorboard logs dir for this run is /home/ubuntu/.yadlt/logs/run82
Accuracy: 0.075: 100%|███████████| 1/1 [00:04<00:00, 4.08s/it]
```

```
Test set accuracy: 0.0773999989033
As can be seen the accuracy again came down so the optimal number of
iterations peaks somewhere between 20 and 40
```

Effect of the number of neurons in an RBM layer in a DBN

Let's look at how changing the number of neurons in an RBM layer affects the test set's accuracy:

An RBM layer with 512 neurons

The following is the output of a DBN with 512 neurons in an RBM layer. The reconstruction loss has come down and the test set's accuracy has come down as well:

```
Reconstruction loss: 0.128517: 100%|███████████| 5/5 [01:32&lt;00:00,
19.25s/it]
Start deep belief net finetuning...
Tensorboard logs dir for this run is /home/ubuntu/.yadlt/logs/run55
Accuracy: 0.0758: 100%|███████████| 1/1 [00:06&lt;00:00, 6.40s/it]
Test set accuracy: 0.0689999982715
```

Notice how the accuracy and test set accuracy both have come down. This means increasing the number of neurons doesn't necessarily improve the accuracy.

An RBM layer with 128 neurons

A 128-neuron RBM layer leads to higher test set accuracy but a lower overall accuracy:

```
Reconstruction loss: 0.180337: 100%|███████████| 5/5 [00:32&lt;00:00,
6.44s/it]
 Start deep belief net finetuning...
 Tensorboard logs dir for this run is /home/ubuntu/.yadlt/logs/run57
 Accuracy: 0.0698: 100%|███████████| 1/1 [00:03&lt;00:00, 3.16s/it]
 Test set accuracy: 0.0763999968767
```

Comparing the accuracy metrics

As we have trained the neural network with multiple neuron numbers in RBM layers, let's compare metrics:

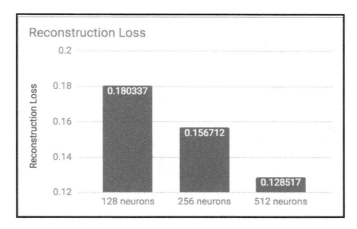

Reconstruction loss reduces as a function of the number of neurons, as shown in the preceding figure.

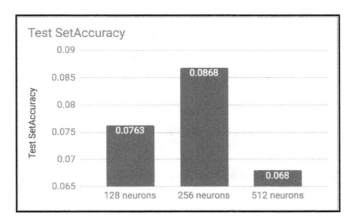

The test set accuracy peaks for 256 neurons and then comes down.

DBNs with two RBM layers

In this section, we will create a DBN with two RBM layers and run it on the MNIST dataset. We will modify the input parameters for the `DeepBeliefNetwork(..)` class:

```
name = 'dbn'
rbm_layers = [256, 256]
finetune_act_func ='relu'
do_pretrain = True
rbm_learning_rate = [0.001, 0.001]
rbm_num_epochs = [5, 5]
rbm_gibbs_k= [1, 1]
rbm_stddev= 0.1
rbm_gauss_visible= False
momentum= 0.5
rbm_batch_size= [32, 32]
finetune_learning_rate = 0.01
finetune_num_epochs = 1
finetune_batch_size = 32
finetune_opt = 'momentum'
finetune_loss_func = 'softmax_cross_entropy'
finetune_dropout = 1
finetune_act_func = tf.nn.sigmoid
```

Notice that some of the parameters have two elements for array so we need to specify these parameters for two layers:

- `rbm_layers = [256, 256]`: Number of neurons in each RBM layer
- `rbm_learning_rate = [0.001, 0001]`: Learning rate for each RBM layer
- `rbm_num_epochs = [5, 5]`: Number of epochs in each layer
- `rbm_batch_size= [32, 32]`: Batch size for each RBM layer

Let's look at the DBN initialization and the training of the model:

```
srbm = dbn.DeepBeliefNetwork(
 name=name, do_pretrain=do_pretrain,
 rbm_layers=rbm_layers,
 finetune_act_func=finetune_act_func, rbm_learning_rate=rbm_learning_rate,
 rbm_num_epochs=rbm_num_epochs, rbm_gibbs_k = rbm_gibbs_k,
 rbm_gauss_visible=rbm_gauss_visible, rbm_stddev=rbm_stddev,
 momentum=momentum, rbm_batch_size=rbm_batch_size,
finetune_learning_rate=finetune_learning_rate,
 finetune_num_epochs=finetune_num_epochs,
finetune_batch_size=finetune_batch_size,
```

```
  finetune_opt=finetune_opt, finetune_loss_func=finetune_loss_func,
  finetune_dropout=finetune_dropout
  )

  if do_pretrain:
    srbm.pretrain(trainX, validX)

  #
  finetuning
  print('Start deep belief net finetuning...')
  srbm.fit(trainX, trainY, validX, validY)
```

Test the model:

```
print('Test set accuracy: {}'.format(srbm.score(testX, testY)))
```

The complete code listing can be found at:
https://github.com/ml-resources/neuralnetwork-programming/blob/
ed1/ch08/implementation/boltzmann/run_dbn_mnist_two_layers.py.

The following is the output of the preceding listing:

```
Reconstruction loss: 0.156286: 100%|████████████| 5/5 [01:03&lt;00:00,
13.04s/it]
Training layer 2...
Tensorboard logs dir for this run is /home/ubuntu/.yadlt/logs/run73
Reconstruction loss: 0.127524: 100%|████████████| 5/5 [00:23&lt;00:00,
4.87s/it]
Start deep belief net finetuning...
Tensorboard logs dir for this run is /home/ubuntu/.yadlt/logs/run74
Accuracy: 0.1496: 100%|████████████| 1/1 [00:05&lt;00:00, 5.53s/it]
Test set accuracy: 0.140300005674
```

As can be seen from the preceding listing, the test set accuracy is better than the single RBM layer DBN.

Classifying the NotMNIST dataset with a DBN

Let's look at the NotMNIST dataset, which we explored in Chapter 2, *Deep Feedforward Networks*, in the *Implementing feedforward networks* section with images, and see how our DBN works for that dataset.

We will leverage the same pickle file, notMNIST.pickle, created in Chapter 2, *Deep Feedforward Networks*. The initialization parameters and imports are listed here:

```
import tensorflow as tf
import numpy as np
import cPickle as pickle

from common.models.boltzmann import dbn
from common.utils import datasets, utilities


flags = tf.app.flags
FLAGS = flags.FLAGS
pickle_file = '../notMNIST.pickle'

image_size = 28
num_of_labels = 10

RELU = 'RELU'
RELU6 = 'RELU6'
CRELU = 'CRELU'
SIGMOID = 'SIGMOID'
ELU = 'ELU'
SOFTPLUS = 'SOFTPLUS'
```

Implementation remains more or less similar to the MNIST dataset. The main implementation listing is given here:

```
if __name__ == '__main__':
    utilities.random_seed_np_tf(-1)
    with open(pickle_file, 'rb') as f:
        save = pickle.load(f)
        training_dataset = save['train_dataset']
        training_labels = save['train_labels']
        validation_dataset = save['valid_dataset']
        validation_labels = save['valid_labels']
        test_dataset = save['test_dataset']
        test_labels = save['test_labels']
```

```
        del save  # hint to help gc free up memory
        print 'Training set', training_dataset.shape, training_labels.shape
        print 'Validation set', validation_dataset.shape,
validation_labels.shape
        print 'Test set', test_dataset.shape, test_labels.shape

    train_dataset, train_labels = reformat(training_dataset,
training_labels)
    valid_dataset, valid_labels = reformat(validation_dataset,
validation_labels)
    test_dataset, test_labels = reformat(test_dataset, test_labels)

    #trainX, trainY, validX, validY, testX, testY =
datasets.load_mnist_dataset(mode='supervised')
    trainX = train_dataset
    trainY = train_labels

    validX = valid_dataset
    validY = valid_labels
    testX = test_dataset
    testY = test_labels

    finetune_act_func = tf.nn.relu
    rbm_layers = [256]
    do_pretrain = True

    name = 'dbn'
    rbm_layers = [256]
    finetune_act_func ='relu'
    do_pretrain = True

    rbm_learning_rate = [0.001]

    rbm_num_epochs = [1]
    rbm_gibbs_k= [1]
    rbm_stddev= 0.1
    rbm_gauss_visible= False
    momentum= 0.5
    rbm_batch_size= [32]
    finetune_learning_rate = 0.01
    finetune_num_epochs = 1
    finetune_batch_size = 32
    finetune_opt = 'momentum'
    finetune_loss_func = 'softmax_cross_entropy'

    finetune_dropout = 1
    finetune_act_func = tf.nn.sigmoid
```

```
    srbm = dbn.DeepBeliefNetwork(
        name=name, do_pretrain=do_pretrain,
        rbm_layers=rbm_layers,
        finetune_act_func=finetune_act_func,
rbm_learning_rate=rbm_learning_rate,
        rbm_num_epochs=rbm_num_epochs, rbm_gibbs_k = rbm_gibbs_k,
        rbm_gauss_visible=rbm_gauss_visible, rbm_stddev=rbm_stddev,
        momentum=momentum, rbm_batch_size=rbm_batch_size,
finetune_learning_rate=finetune_learning_rate,
        finetune_num_epochs=finetune_num_epochs,
finetune_batch_size=finetune_batch_size,
        finetune_opt=finetune_opt, finetune_loss_func=finetune_loss_func,
        finetune_dropout=finetune_dropout
    )

    if do_pretrain:
        srbm.pretrain(trainX, validX)

    # finetuning
    print('Start deep belief net finetuning...')
    srbm.fit(trainX, trainY, validX, validY)

    # Test the model
    print('Test set accuracy: {}'.format(srbm.score(testX, testY)))
```

The complete code listing can be found at:
https://github.com/ml-resources/neuralnetwork-programming/blob/
ed1/ch08/implementation/boltzmann/run_dbn_nomnist.py.

The output of the preceding listing will point the performance of our model for the NotMNIST dataset:

```
Reconstruction loss: 0.546223: 100%|███████████| 1/1 [00:00&lt;00:00,
5.51it/s]
Start deep belief net finetuning...
Tensorboard logs dir for this run is /home/ubuntu/.yadlt/logs/run76
Accuracy: 0.126: 100%|███████████| 1/1 [00:00&lt;00:00, 8.83it/s]
Test set accuracy: 0.180000007153
```

As can be seen, this network performed much better than the MNIST dataset.

Summary

In this chapter, we explored DBNs and looked at how these could be used to build classification pipelines using one or more RBM layers. We looked at various parameters within the RBM layer and their effects on accuracy, reconstruction loss, and test set accuracy. We also looked at single layer and multilayer DBNs using one or more RBMs.

In the next chapter we look at Generative models and how they differ from discriminative models.

8
Autoencoders

An autoencoder is a type of neural network that is trained to attempt to copy its input to its output. It has a hidden layer (let's call it h) that describes a code used to represent the input. The network may be viewed as consisting of two parts:

- **Encoder function**: $h = f(x)$
- **Decoder that produces a reconstruction**: $r = g(h)$

The following figure shows a basic autoencoder with input n and a hidden layer with neurons m:

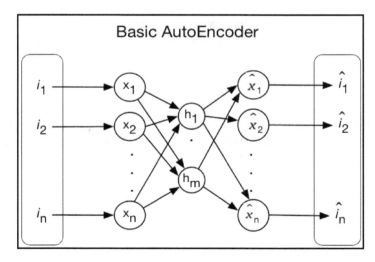

Basic representation of an autoencoder

Autoencoders are designed to be unable to learn to copy perfectly. They are restricted in ways that allow them to copy only approximately, and to copy only input that resembles the training data. As the model is forced to prioritize which aspects of the input should be copied, it often learns useful properties of the data.

The following topics will be covered in this chapter:

- Autoencoder algorithms
- Under-complete autoencoders
- Basic autoencoders
- Additive Gaussian Noise autoencoders
- Sparse autoencoders

Autoencoder algorithms

In the following notation, x is the input, y is the encoded data, z is the decoded data, σ is a nonlinear activation function (sigmoid or hyperbolic tangent, usually), and f(x;θ) means a function of x parameterized by θ.

The model can be summarized in the following way:

The input data is mapped to the hidden layer (encoding). The mapping is usually an affine (allowing for or preserving parallel relationships.) transformation followed by a non-linearity:

```
y = f(x;θ) = σ(Wx+b)y = f(x;θ) =σ(Wx+b)
```

The hidden layer is mapped to the output layer, which is also called **decoding**. The mapping is an affine transformation (affine transformation is a linear mapping method that preserves points, straight lines, and planes) optionally followed by a non linearity. The following equation explains this:

```
z = g(y;θ′) = g(f(x;θ);θ′) = σ(W′y+b′)
```

In order to reduce the size of the model, tied weights can be used, which means that the decoder weights matrix is constrained and can be the transpose of the encoder weights matrix, $\theta'=\theta^T$.

The hidden layer can have a lower or higher dimensionality than that of the input/output layers.

In the case of lower dimensionality, the decoder reconstructs the original input from a lower-dimensional representation of it (also called **under-complete representation**). For the overall algorithm to work, the encoder should learn to provide a low-dimensional representation that captures the essence of the data (that is, the main factors of variations in the distribution). It is forced to find a good way to summarize the data.

 Reference: `http://blackecho.github.io/blog/machine-learning/2016/` `02/29/denoising-autoencoder-tensorflow.html`.

Under-complete autoencoders

One of the ways to obtain useful features from the autoencoder is done by constraining h to have a smaller dimension than input x. An autoencoder with a code dimension less than the input dimension is called under-complete.

Learning a representation that is under-complete forces the autoencoder to capture the most salient features of the training data.

The learning process is described as minimizing a loss function, `L(x, g(f(x)))`, where `L` is a loss function penalizing `g(f (x))` for being dissimilar from x, such as the mean squared error.

Dataset

We are planning to use the MNIST dataset in the `idx3` format as input to train our autoencoders. We will be testing the autoencoder on the first 100 images. Let's first plot the original images:

```python
from tensorflow.examples.tutorials.mnist import input_data
import matplotlib.pyplot as plt


mnist = input_data.read_data_sets('MNIST_data', one_hot = True)

class OriginalImages:

    def __init__(self):
        pass

    def main(self):
        X_train, X_test = self.standard_scale(mnist.train.images,
mnist.test.images)

        original_imgs = X_test[:100]
        plt.figure(1, figsize=(10, 10))

        for i in range(0, 100):
            im = original_imgs[i].reshape((28, 28))
            ax = plt.subplot(10, 10, i + 1)
            for label in (ax.get_xticklabels() + ax.get_yticklabels()):
                label.set_fontsize(8)

            plt.imshow(im, cmap="gray", clim=(0.0, 1.0))
        plt.suptitle(' Original Images', fontsize=15, y=0.95)
        plt.savefig('figures/original_images.png')
        plt.show()


def main():
    auto = OriginalImages()
    auto.main()

if __name__ == '__main__':
    main()
```

The output of the preceding is the following figure:

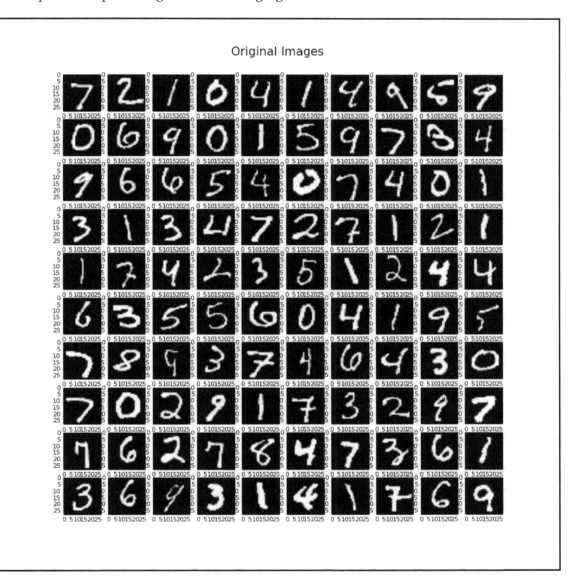

Plot of original MNIST images

Basic autoencoders

Let's look at a basic example of an autoencoder that also happens to be a basic autoencoder. First, we will create an `AutoEncoder` class and initialize it with the following parameters passed to `__init__()`:

- `num_input`: Number of input samples
- `num_hidden`: Number of neurons in the hidden layer
- `transfer_function=tf.nn.softplus`: Transfer function
- `optimizer = tf.train.AdamOptimizer()`: Optimizer

 You can either pass a custom `transfer_function` and `optimizer` or use the default one specified. In our example, we are using softplus as the default `transfer_function` (also called **activation function**): $f(x)=\ln(1+e^x)$.

Autoencoder initialization

First, we initialize the class variables and weights:

```
self.num_input = num_input
self.num_hidden = num_hidden
self.transfer = transfer_function
network_weights = self._initialize_weights()
self.weights = network_weights
```

Here, the `_initialize_weigths()` function is a local function that initializes values for the `weights` dictionary:

- `w1` is a 2D tensor with shape `num_input X num_hidden`
- `b1` is a 1D tensor with shape `num_hidden`
- `w2` is a 2D tensor with shape `num_hidden X num_input`
- `b2` is a 2D tensor with shape `num_input`

The following code shows how weights are initialized as a dictionary of TensorFlow variables for two hidden layers:

```
def _initialize_weights(self):
    weights = dict()
    weights['w1'] = tf.get_variable("w1", shape=[self.num_input,
self.num_hidden],
```

```
                    initializer=tf.contrib.layers.xavier_initializer())
    weights['b1'] = tf.Variable(tf.zeros([self.num_hidden],
dtype=tf.float32))
    weights['w2'] = tf.Variable(tf.zeros([self.num_hidden, self.num_input],
        dtype=tf.float32))
    weights['b2'] = tf.Variable(tf.zeros([self.num_input],
dtype=tf.float32))
    return weights
```

Next, we define x_var, hidden_layer, and reconstruction layer:

```
self.x_var = tf.placeholder(tf.float32, [None, self.num_input])
self.hidden_layer = self.transfer(tf.add(tf.matmul(self.x_var,
    self.weights['w1']), self.weights['b1']))
self.reconstruction = tf.add(tf.matmul(self.hidden_layer,
    self.weights['w2']), self.weights['b2'])
```

```
This is followed by the cost function and the Optimizer
# cost function
self.cost = 0.5 * tf.reduce_sum(
    tf.pow(tf.subtract(self.reconstruction, self.x_var), 2.0))
self.optimizer = optimizer.minimize(self.cost)
```

$$\text{cost} = \frac{1}{2}\sqrt{\sum_{0}^{m-1}\sum_{0}^{n-1}(\hat{x}-x)^2}$$

Cost function

Instantiate the global variables initializer and pass it to TensorFlow session.

```
initializer = tf.global_variables_initializer()
self.session = tf.Session()
self.session.run(initializer)
```

AutoEncoder class

Th following code shows AutoEncoder class. This class with be instantiated for samples in next few sections to create autoencoders:

```
import tensorflow as tf

class AutoEncoder:

    def __init__(self, num_input, num_hidden,
        transfer_function=tf.nn.softplus,
```

```
    optimizer = tf.train.AdamOptimizer()):
        self.num_input = num_input
        self.num_hidden = num_hidden
        self.transfer = transfer_function

        network_weights = self._initialize_weights()
        self.weights = network_weights

        # model for reconstruction of the image
        self.x_var = tf.placeholder(tf.float32, [None, self.num_input])
        self.hidden_layer = self.transfer(tf.add(tf.matmul(self.x_var,
            self.weights['w1']), self.weights['b1']))
        self.reconstruction = tf.add(tf.matmul(self.hidden_layer,
            self.weights['w2']), self.weights['b2'])

        # cost function
        self.cost =
            0.5 * tf.reduce_sum(tf.pow(tf.subtract(self.reconstruction,
            self.x_var), 2.0))
        self.optimizer = optimizer.minimize(self.cost)

        initializer = tf.global_variables_initializer()
        self.session = tf.Session()
        self.session.run(initializer)

    def _initialize_weights(self):
        weights = dict()
        weights['w1'] = tf.get_variable("w1",
                        shape=[self.num_input,
                        self.num_hidden],
                        initializer=
                            tf.contrib.layers.xavier_initializer())
        weights['b1'] = tf.Variable(tf.zeros([self.num_hidden],
                            dtype=tf.float32))
        weights['w2'] = tf.Variable(
            tf.zeros([self.num_hidden, self.num_input],
            dtype=tf.float32))
        weights['b2'] = tf.Variable(tf.zeros(
                        [self.num_input], dtype=tf.float32))
        return weights

    def partial_fit(self, X):
        cost, opt = self.session.run((self.cost, self.optimizer),
            feed_dict={self.x_var: X})
        return cost

    def calculate_total_cost(self, X):
        return self.session.run(self.cost, feed_dict = {self.x_var: X})
```

```
    def transform(self, X):
        return self.session.run(self.hidden_layer,
          feed_dict={self.x_var: X})

    def generate(self, hidden = None):
        if hidden is None:
            hidden = self.session.run(
              tf.random_normal([1, self.num_hidden]))
        return self.session.run(self.reconstruction,
                feed_dict={self.hidden_layer: hidden})

    def reconstruct(self, X):
        return self.session.run(self.reconstruction,
                            feed_dict={self.x_var: X})

    def get_weights(self):
        return self.session.run(self.weights['w1'])

    def get_biases(self):
        return self.session.run(self.weights['b1'])
```

Basic autoencoders with MNIST data

Let's use the autoencoder with MNIST data: `mnist = input_data.read_data_sets('MNIST_data', one_hot = True)`.

Use StandardScalar from Scikit Learn's `sklearn.preprocessing` module to extract testmnist.test.images and training images `mnist.train.images`:

```
X_train, X_test = self.standard_scale(mnist.train.images,
mnist.test.images).
```

 The preprocessing module provides a utility class, `StandardScaler`, which implements the Transformer API. This computes and transforms the mean and standard deviation of a training set. It reapplies the same transformation to the testing set. By default, Scalar centers the mean and makes the variance one.

It is possible to disable either centering or scaling by passing `with_mean=False` or `with_std=False` to the constructor of StandardScaler.

Next, we define an instance of the AutoEncoder class listed earlier:

```
n_samples = int(mnist.train.num_examples)
training_epochs = 5
batch_size = 128
display_step = 1

autoencoder = AutoEncoder(n_input = 784,
    n_hidden = 200,
    transfer_function = tf.nn.softplus,
    optimizer = tf.train.AdamOptimizer(learning_rate = 0.001))
```

Notice that the autoencoder includes the following:

- Number of input neurons is 784
- Number of neurons in the hidden layer is 200
- Activation function is tf.nn.softplus
- Optimizer is tf.train.AdamOptimizer

Next, we iterate over the training data and display the cost function:

```
for epoch in range(training_epochs):
    avg_cost = 0.
    total_batch = int(n_samples / batch_size)
    # Loop over all batches
    for i in range(total_batch):
        batch_xs = self.get_random_block_from_data(X_train, batch_size)

        # Fit training using batch data
        cost = autoencoder.partial_fit(batch_xs)
        # Compute average loss
        avg_cost += cost / n_samples * batch_size

    # Display logs per epoch step
    if epoch % display_step == 0:
        print("Epoch:", '%04d' % (epoch + 1), "cost=",
"{:.9f}".format(avg_cost))
```

Print the total cost:

```
print("Total cost: " + str(autoencoder.calc_total_cost(X_test)))
```

The output of the epochs is listed as follows; as expected, the cost converges with each iteration:

```
('Epoch:', '0001', 'cost=', '20432.278386364')
('Epoch:', '0002', 'cost=', '13542.435997727')
('Epoch:', '0003', 'cost=', '10630.662196023')
('Epoch:', '0004', 'cost=', '10717.897946591')
('Epoch:', '0005', 'cost=', '9354.191921023')
Total cost: 824850.0
```

Basic autoencoder plot of weights

Once the training is done show the plot of weights using the Matplotlib library using code listing:

```
print("Total cost: " + str(autoencoder.calc_total_cost(X_test)))
wts = autoencoder.getWeights()
dim = math.ceil(math.sqrt(autoencoder.n_hidden))
plt.figure(1, figsize=(dim, dim))

for i in range(0, autoencoder.n_hidden):
    im = wts.flatten()[i::autoencoder.n_hidden].reshape((28, 28))
    ax = plt.subplot(dim, dim, i + 1)
    for label in (ax.get_xticklabels() + ax.get_yticklabels()):
        label.set_fontname('Arial')
        label.set_fontsize(8)
    # plt.title('Feature Weights ' + str(i))
    plt.imshow(im, cmap="gray", clim=(-1.0, 1.0))
plt.suptitle('Basic AutoEncoder Weights', fontsize=15, y=0.95)
#plt.title("Test Title", y=1.05)
plt.savefig('figures/basic_autoencoder_weights.png')
plt.show()
```

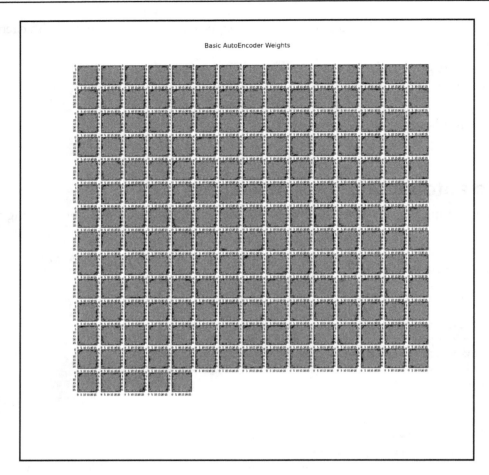

Basic autoencoder weights plot

In the next section, we will look at how images are recreated using the weights shown in the preceding image.

Basic autoencoder recreated images plot

Having recreated the images, let's plot them to get a feel of how they look. First, we will reconstruct the images using the autoencoder instance created earlier:

```
predicted_imgs = autoencoder.reconstruct(X_test[:100])

plt.figure(1, figsize=(10, 10))
```

```
for i in range(0, 100):
    im = predicted_imgs[i].reshape((28, 28))
    ax = plt.subplot(10, 10, i + 1)
    for label in (ax.get_xticklabels() + ax.get_yticklabels()):
            label.set_fontname('Arial')
            label.set_fontsize(8)

    plt.imshow(im, cmap="gray", clim=(0.0, 1.0))
plt.suptitle('Basic AutoEncoder Images', fontsize=15, y=0.95)
plt.savefig('figures/basic_autoencoder_images.png')
plt.show()
```

Let's look at the created images from the neural network:

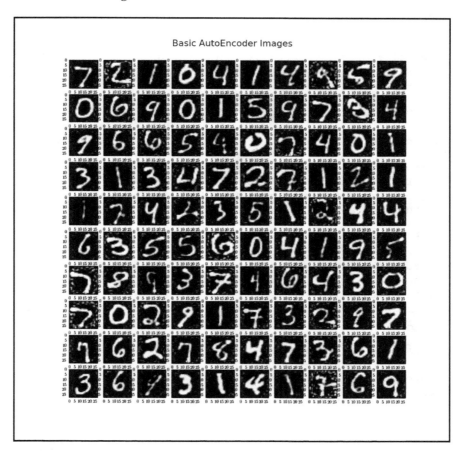

Basic autoencoder plot of output images

Basic autoencoder full code listing

The full code listing can be found here or can also be downloaded from GitHub--`https://github.com/rajdeepd/neuralnetwork-programming/blob/ed1/ch07/basic_autoencoder_example.py`:

```python
import numpy as np

import sklearn.preprocessing as prep
import tensorflow as tf
from tensorflow.examples.tutorials.mnist import input_data
from autencoder_models.auto_encoder import AutoEncoder
import math
import matplotlib.pyplot as plt


mnist = input_data.read_data_sets('MNIST_data', one_hot = True)

class BasicAutoEncoder:

    def __init__(self):
        pass

    def standard_scale(self,X_train, X_test):
        preprocessor = prep.StandardScaler().fit(X_train)
        X_train = preprocessor.transform(X_train)
        X_test = preprocessor.transform(X_test)
        return X_train, X_test

    def get_random_block_from_data(self,data, batch_size):
        start_index = np.random.randint(0, len(data) - batch_size)
        return data[start_index:(start_index + batch_size)]

    def main(self):
        X_train, X_test = self.standard_scale(mnist.train.images,
mnist.test.images)

        n_samples = int(mnist.train.num_examples)
        training_epochs = 5
        batch_size = 128
        display_step = 1

        autoencoder = AutoEncoder(n_input = 784,
                                  n_hidden = 200,
                                  transfer_function = tf.nn.softplus,
                                  optimizer = tf.train.AdamOptimizer(
                                    learning_rate = 0.001))
```

```
        for epoch in range(training_epochs):
            avg_cost = 0.
            total_batch = int(n_samples / batch_size)
            # Loop over all batches
            for i in range(total_batch):
                batch_xs = self.get_random_block_from_data(X_train,
batch_size)

                # Fit training using batch data
                cost = autoencoder.partial_fit(batch_xs)
                # Compute average loss
                avg_cost += cost / n_samples * batch_size

            # Display logs per epoch step
            if epoch % display_step == 0:
                print("Epoch:", '%04d' % (epoch + 1), "cost=",
"{:.9f}".format(avg_cost))

        print("Total cost: " + str(autoencoder.calc_total_cost(X_test)))

        wts = autoencoder.getWeights()
        dim = math.ceil(math.sqrt(autoencoder.n_hidden))
        plt.figure(1, figsize=(dim, dim))

        for i in range(0, autoencoder.n_hidden):
            im = wts.flatten()[i::autoencoder.n_hidden].reshape((28, 28))
            ax = plt.subplot(dim, dim, i + 1)
            for label in (ax.get_xticklabels() + ax.get_yticklabels()):
                label.set_fontname('Arial')
                label.set_fontsize(8)
            # plt.title('Feature Weights ' + str(i))
            plt.imshow(im, cmap="gray", clim=(-1.0, 1.0))
        plt.suptitle('Basic AutoEncoder Weights', fontsize=15, y=0.95)
        #plt.title("Test Title", y=1.05)
        plt.savefig('figures/basic_autoencoder_weights.png')
        plt.show()

        predicted_imgs = autoencoder.reconstruct(X_test[:100])

        plt.figure(1, figsize=(10, 10))

        for i in range(0, 100):
            im = predicted_imgs[i].reshape((28, 28))
            ax = plt.subplot(10, 10, i + 1)
            for label in (ax.get_xticklabels() + ax.get_yticklabels()):
                    label.set_fontname('Arial')
                    label.set_fontsize(8)
```

```
                plt.imshow(im, cmap="gray", clim=(0.0, 1.0))
            plt.suptitle('Basic AutoEncoder Images', fontsize=15, y=0.95)
            plt.savefig('figures/basic_autoencoder_images.png')
            plt.show()

def main():
    auto = BasicAutoEncoder()
    auto.main()

if __name__ == '__main__':
    main()
```

Basic autoencoder summary

The autoencoder created a basic approximation of MNSIT images using 200 neuron hidden layers. The following diagram shows nine images and how they were transformed into approximations using a basic autoencoder:

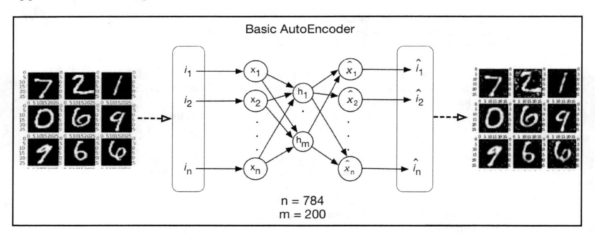

Basic autoencoder input and output representation

In the next section, we will look at a more advanced autoencoder, an **Additive Gaussian Noise AutoEncoder**.

Additive Gaussian Noise autoencoder

What are Denoising autoencoders? They are very similar to the basic model we saw in previous sections, the difference is that, the input is corrupted before being passed to the network. By matching the original version (not the corrupted one) with the reconstruction at training time, this autoencoder gets trained to reconstruct the original input image from the corrupted image. The ability to reconstruct original image from corrupted image makes autoencoder very smart.

An additive noise autoencoder uses the following equation to add corruption to incoming data:

$$x_{corr} = x + scale*random\_normal(n)$$

The following is the detail describe about the preceding equation:

- x is the original image
- *scale* is the multiplier for a random normal number generated from n
- n is the number of training samples
- x_{corr} is the corrupted output

Autoencoder class

We initialize the autoencoder defined in `class AdditiveGaussianNoiseAutoEncoder` by passing following parameters:

- `num_input`: Number of input samples
- `num_hidden`: Number of neurons in the hidden layer
- `transfer_function=tf.nn.sigmoid`: Transfer function
- `optimizer = tf.train.AdamOptimizer()`: Optimizer
- `scale=0.1`: Scale for corruption of the image

```
def __init__(self, num_input, num_hidden,
            transfer_function=tf.nn.sigmoid,
            optimizer=tf.train.AdamOptimizer(),
            scale=0.1):
```

Assign the passed parameters to the instance variables:

```
self.num_input = num_input
self.num_hidden = num_hidden
self.transfer = transfer_function
self.scale = tf.placeholder(tf.float32)
self.training_scale = scale
n_weights = self._initialize_weights()
self.weights = n_weights
```

Initialize the hidden layer `hidden_layer` and the reconstruction layer `reconstruction`:

```
self.x = tf.placeholder(tf.float32, [None, self.num_input])
self.hidden_layer = self.transfer(
        tf.add(tf.matmul(
                self.x + scale * tf.random_normal((n_input,)),
                self.weights['w1']),
                self.weights['b1']))
self.reconstruction = tf.add(
                tf.matmul(self.hidden_layer, self.weights['w2']),
                self.weights['b2'])
```

Define the cost function and the optimizer:

```
self.cost = 0.5 * tf.reduce_sum(tf.pow(tf.subtract(
                        self.reconstruction, self.x), 2.0))
self.optimizer = optimizer.minimize(self.cost)
```

The cost function remains the same as the basic autoencoder

$$\text{cost} = \frac{1}{2}\sqrt{\sum_{0}^{m-1}\sum_{0}^{n-1}(\hat{x}-x)^2}$$

Cost function of additive Gaussian autoencoder

Finally, we initialize global variables, create a TensorFlow session, and run it to execute the `init` graph:

```
init = tf.global_variables_initializer()
self.session = tf.Session()
self.session.run(init)
```

In the next section, we will look at how this autoencoder will be used to encode MNIST data.

Additive Gaussian Autoencoder with the MNIST dataset

First, we load the train and test datasets, `X_train` and `X_test`:

```
mnist = input_data.read_data_sets('MNIST_data', one_hot=True)

def get_random_block_from_data(data, batch_size):
    start_index = np.random.randint(0, len(data) - batch_size)
    return data[start_index:(start_index + batch_size)]

X_train = mnist.train.images
X_test = mnist.test.images
```

Define the variables for the number of samples, `n_samples`, `training_epoch`, and `batch_size` for each iteration of the training and `display_step`:

```
n_samples = int(mnist.train.num_examples)
training_epochs = 2
batch_size = 128
display_step = 1
```

Instantiate the autoencoder and the optimizer. The autoencoder has 200 hidden units and uses sigmoid as the `transfer_function`:

```
autoencoder = AdditiveGaussianNoiseAutoEncoder(n_input=784,
                                               n_hidden=200,
transfer_function=tf.nn.sigmoid,
optimizer=tf.train.AdamOptimizer(learning_rate=0.001),
                                               scale=0.01)
```

Training the model

Once the neural network layers have been defined we train the model by calling method

`autoencoder.partial_fit(batch_xs)` for each batch of data:

```
for epoch in range(training_epochs):
    avg_cost = 0.
    total_batch = int(n_samples / batch_size)
    # Loop over all batches
    for i in range(total_batch):
        batch_xs = get_random_block_from_data(X_train, batch_size)

        # Fit training using batch data
        cost = autoencoder.partial_fit(batch_xs)
        # Compute average loss
        avg_cost += cost / n_samples * batch_size

    # Display logs per epoch step
    if epoch % display_step == 0:
        print("Epoch:", '%04d' % (epoch + 1), "cost=", avg_cost)

print("Total cost: " + str(autoencoder.calc_total_cost(X_test)))
```

The cost of each epoch is printed:

```
('Epoch:', '0001', 'cost=', 1759.873304261363)
('Epoch:', '0002', 'cost=', 686.85984829545475)
('Epoch:', '0003', 'cost=', 460.52834446022746)
('Epoch:', '0004', 'cost=', 355.10590241477308)
('Epoch:', '0005', 'cost=', 297.99104825994351)
```

The total cost of training is as follows:

```
Total cost: 21755.4
```

Plotting the weights

Let's plot the weights visually and plot them using Matplotlib:

```
wts = autoencoder.get_weights()
dim = math.ceil(math.sqrt(autoencoder.num_hidden))
plt.figure(1, figsize=(dim, dim))
for i in range(0, autoencoder.num_hidden):
    im = wts.flatten()[i::autoencoder.num_hidden].reshape((28, 28))
    ax = plt.subplot(dim, dim, i + 1)
    for label in (ax.get_xticklabels() + ax.get_yticklabels()):
```

```
        label.set_fontsize(8)
    #plt.title('Feature Weights ' + str(i))

    plt.imshow(im, cmap="gray", clim=(-1.0, 1.0))
plt.suptitle('Additive Gaussian Noise AutoEncoder Weights', fontsize=15,
y=0.95)
plt.savefig('figures/additive_gaussian_weights.png')
plt.show()
```

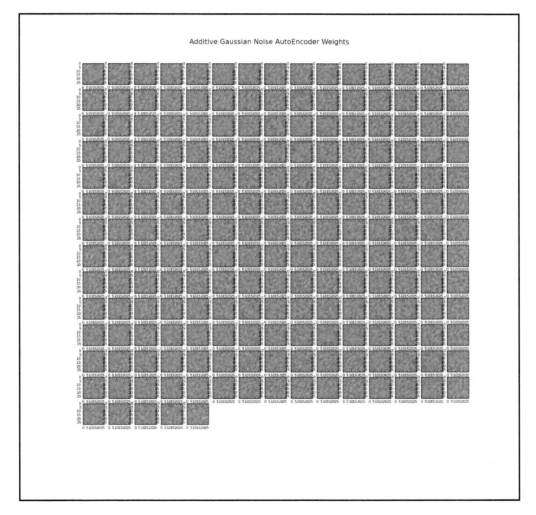

Weights of the neurons in hidden layers for the Additive Gaussian Auto Encoder

Plotting the reconstructed images

The last step is to print the reconstructed images to give us visual proof of how the encoder is able to reconstruct the images based on the weights:

```
predicted_imgs = autoencoder.reconstruct(X_test[:100])

# plot the reconstructed images
plt.figure(1, figsize=(10, 10))
plt.title('Autoencoded Images')
for i in range(0, 100):
    im = predicted_imgs[i].reshape((28, 28))
    ax = plt.subplot(10, 10, i + 1)
    for label in (ax.get_xticklabels() + ax.get_yticklabels()):
        label.set_fontname('Arial')
        label.set_fontsize(8)

    plt.imshow(im, cmap="gray", clim=(0.0, 1.0))
plt.suptitle('Additive Gaussian Noise AutoEncoder Images', fontsize=15,
y=0.95)
plt.savefig('figures/additive_gaussian_images.png')
plt.show()
```

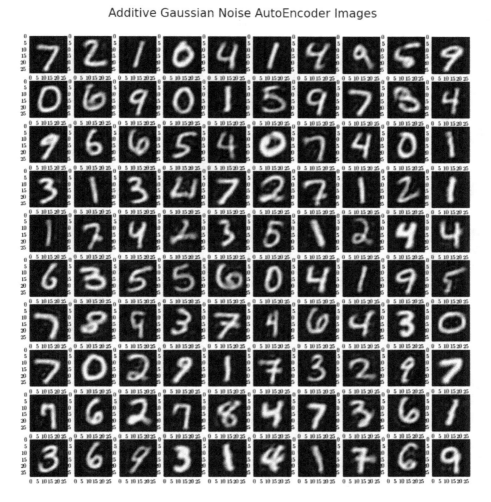

Reconstructed images using the Additive Gaussian Auto Encoder

Additive Gaussian autoencoder full code listing

The following is the code of the Additive Gaussian autoencoder:

```
import numpy as np
import tensorflow as tf
def xavier_init(fan_in, fan_out, constant = 1):
    low = -constant * np.sqrt(6.0 / (fan_in + fan_out))
    high = constant * np.sqrt(6.0 / (fan_in + fan_out))
    return tf.random_uniform((fan_in, fan_out), minval = low, maxval =
high, dtype = tf.float32)

class AdditiveGaussianNoiseAutoEncoder(object):
    def __init__(self, num_input, num_hidden,
                transfer_function=tf.nn.sigmoid,
                optimizer=tf.train.AdamOptimizer(),
                scale=0.1):
        self.num_input = num_input
        self.num_hidden = num_hidden
        self.transfer = transfer_function
        self.scale = tf.placeholder(tf.float32)
        self.training_scale = scale
        n_weights = self._initialize_weights()
        self.weights = n_weights
       # model
</span>        self.x = tf.placeholder(tf.float32, [None, self.num_input])
        self.hidden_layer = self.transfer(
           tf.add(tf.matmul(
                self.x + scale * tf.random_normal((n_input,)),
                self.weights['w1']),
                self.weights['b1']))
        self.reconstruction = tf.add(
                        tf.matmul(self.hidden_layer, self.weights['w2']),
                        self.weights['b2'])

        # cost
        self.cost = 0.5 * tf.reduce_sum(tf.pow(tf.subtract(
                    self.reconstruction, self.x), 2.0))

        self.optimizer = optimizer.minimize(self.cost)

        init = tf.global_variables_initializer()
        self.session = tf.Session()
        self.session.run(init)

    def _initialize_weights(self):
        weights = dict()
```

```
        weights['w1'] = tf.Variable(xavier_init(self.num_input,
self.num_hidden))
        weights['b1'] = tf.Variable(tf.zeros([self.num_hidden],
dtype=tf.float32))
        weights['w2'] = tf.Variable(tf.zeros([self.num_hidden,
self.num_input],
          dtype=tf.float32))
        weights['b2'] = tf.Variable(tf.zeros([self.num_input],
dtype=tf.float32))
        return weights

    def partial_fit(self, X):
        cost, opt = self.session.run((self.cost, self.optimizer),
            feed_dict={self.x: X,self.scale: self.training_scale})
        return cost

    def kl_divergence(self, p, p_hat):
        return tf.reduce_mean(
          p * tf.log(p) - p * tf.log(p_hat) + (1 - p) * tf.log(1 - p) - (1
- p) *        tf.log(1 - p_hat))

    def calculate_total_cost(self, X):
        return self.session.run(self.cost, feed_dict={self.x: X,
                                          self.scale:
self.training_scale
                                          })

    def transform(self, X):
        return self.session.run(
          self.hidden_layer,
          feed_dict = {self.x: X, self.scale: self.training_scale})

    def generate_value(self, _hidden=None):
        if _hidden is None:
            _hidden = np.random.normal(size=self.weights["b1"])
        return self.session.run(self.reconstruction,
            feed_dict={self.hidden_layer: _hidden})

    def reconstruct(self, X):
        return self.session.run(self.reconstruction,
          feed_dict={self.x: X,self.scale: self.training_scale })

    def get_weights(self):
        return self.session.run(self.weights['w1'])

    def get_biases(self):
        return self.session.run(self.weights['b1'])
```

Comparing basic encoder costs with the Additive Gaussian Noise autoencoder

The following graph shows the cost of two algorithms for each epoch. It can be inferred that the basic autoencoder is much more expensive compared to the Additive Gaussian Noise autoencoder:

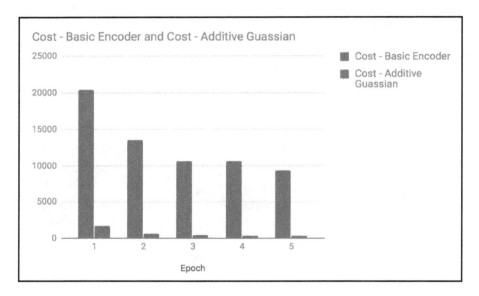

Cost comparison: basic versus Additive Gaussian Noise autoencoder

Additive Gaussian Noise autoencoder summary

You learned how to create an autoencoder with Gaussian noise, which helps in improving the accuracy of the model drastically when compared to the basic autoencoder.

Sparse autoencoder

In this section, we will look at how adding sparsity to the cost function helps in reducing the cost of training. Most of the code remains the same, but the primary changes are in the way the cost function is calculated.

KL divergence

Let's first try to understand KL divergence, which is used to add sparsity to the cost function.

We can think of a neuron as active (or *firing*) if a neuron's output value is close to one, and *inactive* if its output value is close to zero. We would like to constrain the neurons to be inactive most of the time. This discussion assumes a sigmoid activation function. Recall that $a^{(2)}_j$ denotes the activation of the hidden unit j in the autoencoder. This notation does not state explicitly what the input x was that led to this activation. We will write $a^{(2)}_j(x)$ to denote the activation of the hidden unit when the network is given a specific input x.

Further, let $\hat{\rho}_j = \frac{1}{m}\sum_{i=1}^{m}\left[a_j^{(2)}\left(x^{(i)}\right)\right]$ be the average activation of the hidden unit j (averaged over the training set). We would like to (approximately) enforce the constraint $\hat{\rho}_j = \rho$, where ρ is a sparsity parameter, typically a small value close to zero (say, = 0.05). Our aim is that the average activation of each hidden neuron j be close to *0.05* (as an example). To satisfy the preceding constraint, the hidden unit's activation must mostly be close to zero.

To achieve this, an extra penalty term is added to the optimization objective that penalizes it, deviating significantly from ρ:

$$\sum_{j=1}^{s_2} \rho \log \frac{\rho}{\hat{\rho}_j} + (1-\rho)\log \frac{1-\rho}{1-\hat{\rho}_j}$$

Let's take a look at how KL divergence varies as a function of the average activation:

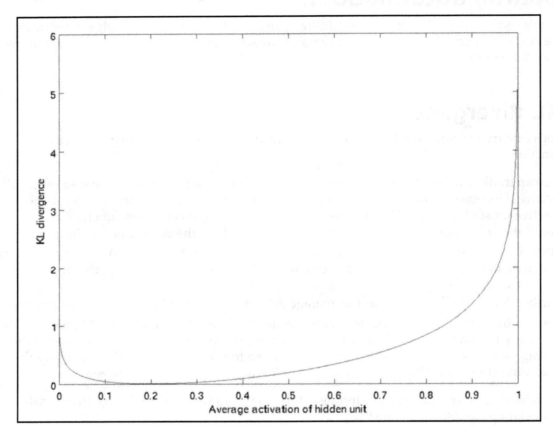

Average activation versus KL divergence plot

KL divergence in TensorFlow

In our implementation of a sparse encoder, we defined KL divergence in a `kl_divergence` function in the `SparseEncoder` class, which is nothing but an implementation of the preceding formula:

```
def kl_divergence(self, p, p_hat):
    return tf.reduce_mean(
            p*(tf.log(p)/tf.log(p_hat)) +
            (1-p)*(tf.log(1-p)/tf.log(1-p_hat)))
```

Cost of a sparse autoencoder based on KL Divergence

The cost function is redefined with two new parameters, `sparse_reg` and `kl_divergence`, when compared to the previous encoders discussed in this chapter:

```
self.cost = 0.5 * tf.reduce_sum(
  tf.pow(tf.subtract(self.reconstruction, self.x), 2.0)) +
    self.sparse_reg * self.kl_divergence(self.sparsity_level,
self.hidden_layer)
```

Complete code listing of the sparse autoencoder

For reference, we have given the code listing for `SparseAutoEncoder` here, with the `kl_divergence` and `cost` discussed earlier:

```
class SparseAutoencoder(object):
    def __init__(self, num_input, num_hidden,
                 transfer_function=tf.nn.softplus,
                 optimizer=tf.train.AdamOptimizer(),
                 scale=0.1):
        self.num_input = num_input
        self.num_hidden = num_hidden
        self.transfer = transfer_function
        self.scale = tf.placeholder(tf.float32)
        self.training_scale = scale
        network_weights = self._initialize_weights()
        self.weights = network_weights
        self.sparsity_level = np.repeat([0.05],
            self.num_hidden).astype(np.float32)
        self.sparse_reg = 0.0

        # model
        self.x = tf.placeholder(tf.float32, [None, self.num_input])
        self.hidden_layer = self.transfer(tf.add(tf.matmul(
            self.x + scale * tf.random_normal((num_input,)),
                                        self.weights['w1']),
                                        self.weights['b1']))
        self.reconstruction = tf.add(tf.matmul(self.hidden_layer,
            self.weights['w2']), self.weights['b2'])

        # cost
        self.cost = 0.5 * tf.reduce_sum(
            tf.pow(tf.subtract(self.reconstruction, self.x), 2.0)) +
            self.sparse_reg * self.kl_divergence(
                self.sparsity_level, self.hidden_layer)
```

```
        self.optimizer = optimizer.minimize(self.cost)

        init = tf.global_variables_initializer()
        self.session = tf.Session()
        self.session.run(init)

    def _initialize_weights(self):
        all_weights = dict()
        all_weights['w1'] = tf.Variable(xavier_init(self.num_input,
            self.num_hidden))
        all_weights['b1'] = tf.Variable(tf.zeros([self.num_hidden],
            dtype = tf.float32))
        all_weights['w2'] = tf.Variable(tf.zeros([self.num_hidden,
                            self.num_input],
                            dtype = tf.float32))
        all_weights['b2'] = tf.Variable(tf.zeros([self.num_input],
            dtype = tf.float32))
        return all_weights

    def partial_fit(self, X):
        cost, opt = self.session.run((self.cost, self.optimizer),
                    feed_dict = {self.x: X,
                                 self.scale: self.training_scale})
        return cost

    def kl_divergence(self, p, p_hat):
        return tf.reduce_mean(p*(tf.log(p)/tf.log(p_hat)) +
            (1-p)*(tf.log(1-p)/tf.log(1-p_hat)))

    def calculate_total_cost(self, X):
        return self.session.run(self.cost, feed_dict = {
            self.x: X,
            self.scale: self.training_scale
        })

    def transform(self, X):
        return self.session.run(self.hidden_layer,
            feed_dict = {self.x: X, self.scale: self.training_scale})

    def generate(self, hidden = None):
        if hidden is None:
            hidden = np.random.normal(size = self.weights["b1"])
            return self.session.run(self.reconstruction,
                feed_dict = {self.hidden_layer: hidden})

    def reconstruct(self, X):
        return self.session.run(self.reconstruction,
            feed_dict = {self.x: X, self.scale: self.training_scale})
```

```
        def get_weights(self):
            return self.session.run(self.weights['w1'])

        def get_biases(self):
            return self.session.run(self.weights['b1'])
```

In the next section we will look at Sparse autoencoder applied to a specific dataset.

Sparse autoencoder on MNIST data

Let's run this encoder on the same dataset that we used in the other examples and compare the results:

```
class SparseAutoEncoderExample:
    def main(self):
        mnist = input_data.read_data_sets('MNIST_data', one_hot = True)

        def get_random_block_from_data(data, batch_size):
            start_index = np.random.randint(0, len(data) - batch_size)
            return data[start_index:(start_index + batch_size)]

        X_train = mnist.train.images
        X_test = mnist.test.images

        n_samples = int(mnist.train.num_examples)
        training_epochs = 5
        batch_size = 128
        display_step = 1

        autoencoder =SparseAutoencoder(num_input=784,
                                num_hidden = 200,
                                transfer_function = tf.nn.sigmoid,
                                optimizer = tf.train.AdamOptimizer(
                                    learning_rate = 0.001),
                                scale = 0.01)

        for epoch in range(training_epochs):
            avg_cost = 0.
            total_batch = int(n_samples / batch_size)
            # Loop over all batches
            for i in range(total_batch):
                batch_xs = get_random_block_from_data(X_train, batch_size)

                # Fit training using batch data
                cost = autoencoder.partial_fit(batch_xs)
```

```
                    # Compute average loss
                    avg_cost += cost / n_samples * batch_size

                # Display logs per epoch step
                if epoch % display_step == 0:
                    print("Epoch:", '%04d' % (epoch + 1), "cost=", avg_cost)

            print("Total cost: " +
                str(autoencoder.calculate_total_cost(X_test)))

            # input weights
            wts = autoencoder.get_weights()
            dim = math.ceil(math.sqrt(autoencoder.num_hidden))
            plt.figure(1, figsize=(dim, dim))
            for i in range(0, autoencoder.num_hidden):
                im = wts.flatten()[i::autoencoder.num_hidden].reshape((28, 28))
                ax = plt.subplot(dim, dim, i + 1)
                for label in (ax.get_xticklabels() + ax.get_yticklabels()):
                    label.set_fontsize(6)
                plt.subplot(dim, dim, i+1)
                plt.imshow(im, cmap="gray", clim=(-1.0, 1.0))
            plt.suptitle('Sparse AutoEncoder Weights', fontsize=15, y=0.95)
            plt.savefig('figures/sparse_autoencoder_weights.png')
            plt.show()

            predicted_imgs = autoencoder.reconstruct(X_test[:100])

            # plot the reconstructed images
            plt.figure(1, figsize=(10, 10))
            plt.title('Sparse Autoencoded Images')
            for i in range(0,100):
                im = predicted_imgs[i].reshape((28,28))
                ax = plt.subplot(10, 10, i + 1)
                for label in (ax.get_xticklabels() + ax.get_yticklabels()):
                    label.set_fontsize(6)

                plt.subplot(10, 10, i+1)
                plt.imshow(im, cmap="gray", clim=(0.0, 1.0))
            plt.suptitle('Sparse AutoEncoder Images', fontsize=15, y=0.95)
            plt.savefig('figures/sparse_autoencoder_images.png')
            plt.show()

def main():
    auto = SparseAutoEncoderExample()
    auto.main()

if __name__ == '__main__':
    main()
```

The output of the preceding code is as follows:

```
('Epoch:', '0001', 'cost=', 1697.039439488638)
('Epoch:', '0002', 'cost=', 667.23002088068188)
('Epoch:', '0003', 'cost=', 450.02947024147767)
('Epoch:', '0004', 'cost=', 351.54360497159115)
('Epoch:', '0005', 'cost=', 293.73473448153396)
Total cost: 21025.2
```

As can be seen, the cost is lower than other encoders, hence KL divergence and sparsity definitely help.

Comparing the Sparse encoder with the Additive Gaussian Noise encoder

The following graph shows how the costs compare for the Additive Gaussian Noise autoencoder and the Sparse autoencoder:

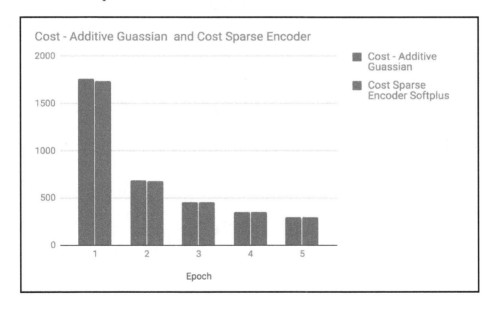

Cost comparison of two autoencoders for five epochs on the MNIST dataset

Summary

In this chapter, you learned three different types of autoencoders: basic, Additive Gaussian Noise, and Sparse. We understood the use cases where they can be useful. We ran them against the MNIST dataset and also compared the cost of the three autoencoders. We also plotted the weights as well as the approximate output.

9
Research in Neural Networks

In this chapter, we will look at some of the active research areas in neural networks. The following problems are analyzed from basic research areas to complex real-life problems:

- Overfitting in neural networks
- Large-scale video processing with a neural network
- Named entity recognition using a twisted neural network
- Bidirectional recurrent neural networks

Avoiding overfitting in neural networks

Let's understand the constituents of overfitting and how to avoid it in neural networks. Nitesh Srivastava, Geoffrey Hinton, et al. published a paper, `https://www.cs.toronto.edu/~hinton/absps/JMLRdropout.pdf`, in 2014, which shows cases on how to avoid overfitting.

Problem statement

Deep neural networks contain nonlinear hidden layers, and this makes them expressive models that can learn very complicated relationships between inputs and outputs. However, these complicated relationships will be the result of sampling noise. These complicated relationships might not exist in test data, leading to overfitting. Many techniques and methods have been developed to reduce this noise. These include stopping the training as soon as performance on a validation set starts getting worse, introducing weight penalties such as L1 and L2 regularization, and soft weight sharing (Nowlan and Hinton, 1992).

Solution

Dropout is a technique that addresses performance issues of some of the other techniques such as averaging across multiple models. It also prevents overfitting and provides a way to combine exponentially many different neural network architectures efficiently. The term dropout means dropping out units (hidden and visible) in a neural network. By dropping a unit out, it means removing it from the network and its incoming and outgoing connections, as shown in the following figure.

The choice of which units to be dropped is usually random. In a simple case, each unit is retained with a probability p independent of other units. The technique to choose p can be a validation set or can be set at 0.5; this value is close to optimal for a wide range of networks and tasks.

For the input units, however, the optimal probability of retention is usually closer to 1 than to 0.5.

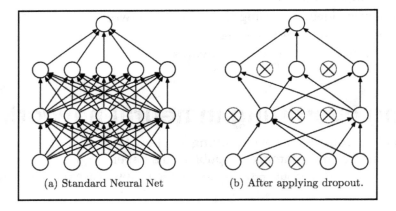

(a) Standard Neural Net   (b) After applying dropout.

Dropout neural net model:

- A standard neural network with two hidden layers
- A thinned neural net produced by applying dropout to the network on the left; crossed units have been dropped

Example of how Dropout can be applied in TensorFlow

```
cell = tf.nn.rnn_cell.LSTMCell(state_size, state_is_tuple=True)
cell = tf.nn.rnn_cell.DropoutWrapper(cell, output_keep_prob=0.5)
cell = tf.nn.rnn_cell.MultiRNNCell([cell] * num_layers,
state_is_tuple=True)
```

As can be seen above a Dropout of 0.5 is applied to the `LSTMCell`, where `output_keep_prob`: unit Tensor or float between 0 and 1, output keep probability; if it is constant and 1, no output dropout will be added.

Results

Let's look at how the dropout strategy affects the accuracy of the model:

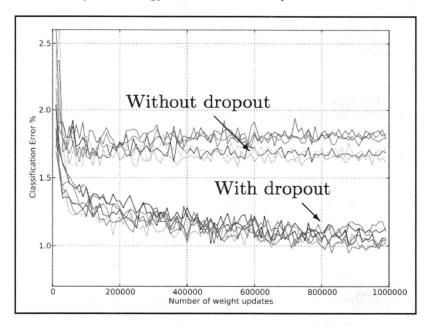

As can be seen, the classification error decreases significantly with dropout.

Large-scale video processing with neural networks

In this paper, `https://static.googleusercontent.com/media/research.google.com/en//pubs/archive/42455.pdf`, the authors explore how CNNs could be used for large-scale video classification. In this use case, the neural networks have access to not only the appearance information in single, static images, but also the complex temporal evolution of the image. There are several challenges in extending and applying CNNs in this setting.

There are very few (or none) video classification benchmarks that match the scale and variety of existing image datasets as videos are significantly more challenging to collect, annotate, and store. To obtain sufficient amount of data needed to train our CNN architectures, authors collected a new Sports-1M dataset. This dataset contains 1 million videos (from YouTube) belonging to a taxonomy of 487 classes of sports. Sports-1M is also available to the research community to support future work in this area.

In this work, the authors treat every video as a bag of short, fixed-sized clips. Each clip contains several contiguous frames in time, hence the connectivity of the network can be extended in a time dimension to learning spatio-temporal features. The authors describe three broad connectivity pattern categories (**Early Fusion**, **Late Fusion**, and **Slow Fusion**). Afterward, we will look at a multiresolution architecture to address the computational efficiency.

The following figure explains various techniques for fusion:

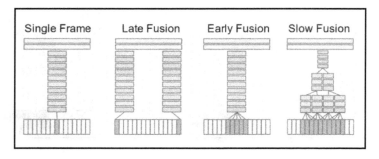

Various fusion techniques to combine frames separated by time

Resolution improvements

The authors used a multiresolution architecture that aimed to strike a compromise by having two separate streams of processing (called Fovea and Context Streams) over two spatial resolutions (see the following figure). A 178 × 178 frame video clip is the input to the network:

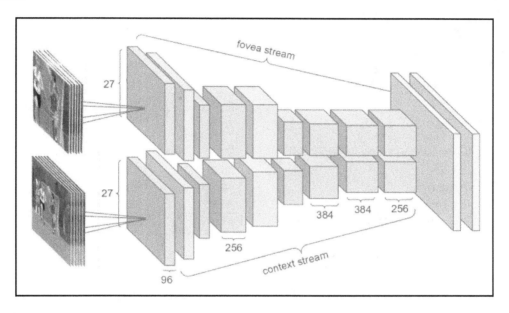

Multiresolution CNN

The **context stream** receives the downsampled frames at half the original spatial resolution (89 × 89 pixels). The **fovea stream** receives the center 89 × 89 region at the original resolution. In this way, the total input dimensionality is halved.

Feature histogram baselines

In addition to comparing CNN architectures with each other, the authors also report the accuracy of a feature-based approach. A standard bag-of-words pipeline was used to extract several types of features at all frames of the videos, followed by discretizing them using k-means vector quantization and accumulating words into histograms with spatial pyramid encoding and soft quantization.

Quantitative results

Sports-1M dataset test set results (200,000 videos and 4,000,000 clips) are summarized in the following table. The approach of multiple networks consistently and significantly outperforms the feature-based baseline. The feature-based approach computes visual words densely over the duration of the video and produces predictions that are based on the complete video-level feature vector, while the authors' networks only see 20 randomly sampled clips individually:

Model	Clip Hit@1	Video Hit@1	Video Hit@5
Feature Histograms + Neural Net	-	55.3	-
Single-Frame	41.1	59.3	77.7
Single-Frame + Multires	**42.4**	**60.0**	**78.5**
Single-Frame Fovea Only	30.0	49.9	72.8
Single-Frame Context Only	38.1	56.0	77.2
Early Fusion	38.9	57.7	76.8
Late Fusion	40.7	59.3	78.7
Slow Fusion	**41.9**	**60.9**	**80.2**
CNN Average (Single+Early+Late+Slow)	41.4	63.9	82.4

Results on the 200,000 videos of the Sports-1M test set. Hit@k values indicate the fraction of test samples that contained at least one of the ground truth labels in the top k predictions.

The approach taken with network topology learns well despite label noise; the training videos are subject to some incorrect annotations and even the correctly-labeled videos often contain a large amount of artifacts such as text, effects, cuts, and logos, none of which we attempted to filter out explicitly.

Named entity recognition using a twisted neural network

In this paper, http://www.cs.cmu.edu/~leili/pubs/lu-baylearn2015-twinet.pdf, the authors look at the problem of recognizing entities in natural language. This is often the first step in question answering, conversations, and a host of other NLP use cases. For a sequence of text tokens, a named entity recognizer identifies chunks of tokens that belong to a predefined category of persons and organizations.

Example of a named entity recognition

IOB tagging system is one of the convention for NER.

The **IOB Tagging** system contains tags of the form:

- B-{CHUNK_TYPE}: for the word in the **B**eginning chunk
- I-{CHUNK_TYPE}: for words **I**nside the chunk
- O: **O**utside any chunk
- B-PERSON : Person Entity
- B-GPE : Geopolitical Entity

Th following text shows example of a names entities in a sentence:

```
John     has lived in Britain  for     14        years    .
B-PERSON O    O    O  B-GPE     O  B-CARDINAL I-CARDINAL O
```

However, it is quite challenging due to two reasons:

- Entity databases are often incomplete (given the number of new organizations being established)
- The same phrase can refer to a different entity (or none entity) depending on the context

Defining Twinet

Twisting RNNs (Twinet) use two parallel branches. Each branch is composed of a recurrent network layer, a nonlinear perceptron layer, and a reversed recurrent network layer. Branches are *twisted*: the order of the layers is reversed in the second branch. The output of all the recurrent layers is collected toward the end.

To recap, a **recurrent neural network** (**RNN**) takes a sequence of input vectors $x1..T$, and recurrently computes hidden states (also called **output labels**):

$$h_t = \sigma(U \cdot x_t + W \cdot ht{-}1)$$

where,

- t is 1..T
- x_t is the external signal
- W are the weights
- h_{t-1} is the hidden layer weights for time step t-1
- h_t weights being calculated for time step t
- U is tan$h$ layer which helps in creating weights for time step t

$\sigma(\cdot)$ is a nonlinear activation function. In the experiments that the authors used, we used **rectified linear units** (**RELU**).

Results

Twinet was compared to Stanford NER and Illinois NER and the results were quite favorable. Here NER stands for60; (**Named Entity Recognizer**).

	P	R	F1
Stanford NER	84.04	80.86	82.42
Illinois NER	85.86	84.20	85.02
Twinet	86.06	86.34	**86.20**

As can be seen from the preceding figure, the Precision-Recall as well as the F1 scores are all higher.

Bidirectional RNNs

In this section, we will look at a new neural network topology that is gaining momentum in the area of NLP.

Schuster and Paliwal have introduced **Bidirectional Recurrent Neural Networks (BRNN)** in 1997. BRNNs help increase the amount of input information available to the network. **Multilayer perceptrons (MLPs)** and **time delay neural networks (TDNNs)** are known to have limitations on the input data flexibility. RNNs also require their input data to be fixed. More advanced topologies like RNNs also have restrictions as the future input information cannot be predicted from the current state. BRNNs, on the contrary, do not need their input data to be fixed. Their future input information is reachable from the current state. The idea of BRNNs is to connect two hidden layers of opposite directions to the same output. With this structure, the output layer is able to get information from past and future states.

BRNNs are useful when the context of the input is needed. As an example, in handwriting recognition, the performance can be enhanced by knowledge of the letters located before and after the current letter.

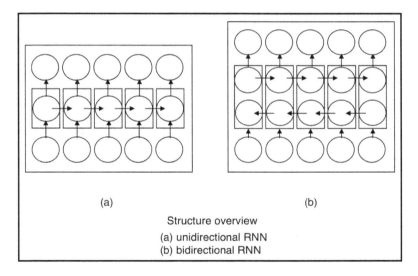

(a)   (b)

Structure overview
(a) unidirectional RNN
(b) bidirectional RNN

This depicts a Bidirectional RNN

BRNN on TIMIT dataset

In this section, we will look at how a BRNN provides higher accuracy results on the TIMIT Dataset for phoneme text classification.

TIMIT is a corpus of phonemically and lexically transcribed speeches of American English speakers of different sexes and dialects. Each transcribed element has been delineated in time. TIMIT was designed to further acoustic-phonetic knowledge and automatic speech recognition systems:

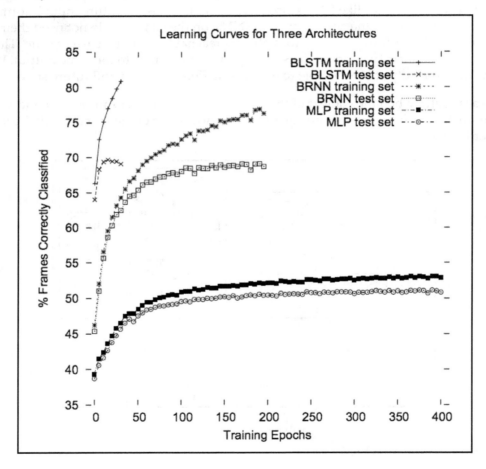

As can be seen from the preceding figure, the BRNN gives higher percent frames accurately as compared to MLP, both for the training set and testing set. BLSTM gives even higher accuracy.

Summary

In this chapter, we addressed some of the areas where research has been done on improving accuracy and avoiding overfitting. We also looked at some of the newer areas such as video classification. While it is outside the scope of this book to cover all the research areas in detail, we sincerely advise you to explore the research websites of Google, Facebook, and Baidu, in addition to Tier 1 ACM and IEEE conferences, to skim through new research being done.

Getting started with TensorFlow

TensorFlow is an open source deep learning library by Google. It provides primitives for defining functions on tensors and automatically computing their derivatives. A tensor can be represented as a multidimensional array of numbers. Scalar, Vector, and Matrix are types of tensors. TensorFlow is mainly used to design computational graphs, build, and train deep learning models. The TensorFlow library does numerical computations using data flow graphs, where the nodes represent mathematical operations and the edges represent the data points (usually multidimensional arrays or tensors that are transmitted between these edges).

Environment setup

It is best to use an IDE such as PyCharm to edit Python code; it provides faster development tools and coding assistance. Code completion and inspection makes coding and debugging faster and simpler, ensuring that you focus on the end goal of programming neural networks.

TensorFlow provides APIs for multiple languages: Python, C++, Java, Go, and so on. We will download a version of TensorFlow that will enable us to write the code for deep learning models in Python. On the TensorFlow installation website, we can find the most common ways and latest instructions to install TensorFlow using virtualenv, pip, and Docker.

The following steps describe how to set up a local development environment:

1. Download the Pycharm community edition.
2. Get the latest Python version on Pycharm.
3. Go to **Preferences**, set up the python interpreter, and install the latest version of TensorFlow:

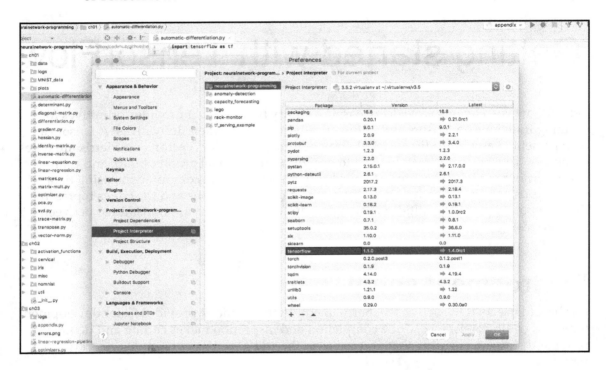

4. TensorFlow will now appear in the installed packages list. Click on **OK**. Now test your installation with a program such as hello world:

```
import TensorFlow  as tf
helloWorld = tf.constant("Hello World!")
sess = tf.Session()
print(sess.run(helloWorld))
```

TensorFlow comparison with Numpy

TensorFlow and Numpy are both N-dimensional array libraries. TensorFlow additionally allows us to create tensor functions and compute derivatives. TensorFlow has become one of the major libraries used for deep learning as it is incredibly efficient and can run on GPUs.

The following program describes how `TensorFlow` and `numpy` can be used to perform similar operations such as creating tensors of a `(3,3)` shape:

```
import TensorFlow  as tf
import numpy as np

tf.InteractiveSession()

# TensorFlow  operations
a = tf.zeros((3,3))
b = tf.ones((3,3))

print(tf.reduce_sum(b, reduction_indices=1).eval())
print(a.get_shape())

# numpy operations
a = np.zeros((3, 3))
b = np.ones((3, 3))
print(np.sum(b, axis=1))
print(a.shape)
```

The output of the preceding code is as follows:

```
[ 3.   3.   3.]
(3, 3)
[ 3.   3.   3.]
(3, 3)
```

Computational graph

TensorFlow is based on building a computational graph. A computational graph is a network of nodes, where each node defines an operation running a function; this can be as plain as addition or subtraction, or as complicated as a multivariate equation. TensorFlow programs are structured in a construction phase that assembles a graph and an execution phase that utilizes a session object to execute operations in the graph.

An operation is referred to as the op and can return zero or more tensors, which can be used later in the graph. Each op can be given a constant, array, or n-dimensional matrix.

Graph

The default graph gets instantiated when the TensorFlow library is imported. Constructing a graph object instead of using the default graph is useful when creating multiple models in one file that do not depend on each other. Constants and operations are added to the graph in TensorFlow.

Variables and operations applied outside of `newGraph.as_default()` will get added to the default graph, which is created when the library is imported:

```
newGraph = tf.Graph()
with newGraph.as_default():
    newGraphConst = tf.constant([2., 3.])
```

Session objects

A session in TensorFlow encapsulates the environment in which tensor objects are evaluated. Sessions can have their private variables, queues, and readers that are designated. We should use the close method at the end of the session.

The session has three arguments, which are optional:

- `Target`: The execution engine to connect to
- `graph`: The graph object to be started
- `config`: This is a ConfigProto protocol buffer

To run a single step of the TensorFlow computation, the step function is invoked and necessary dependencies of the graph are executed:

```
# session objects
a = tf.constant(6.0)
b = tf.constant(7.0)

c = a * b
with tf.Session() as sess:
    print(sess.run(c))
    print(c.eval())
```

`sess.run(c)` in the currently active session!

The preceding code gives the following output:

```
42.0, 42.0
```

The `tf.InteractiveSession()` function is an easy way of keeping a default session open in `ipython`. The `sess.run(c)` is an example of a TensorFlow Fetch:

```
session = tf.InteractiveSession()
cons1 = tf.constant(1)
cons2 = tf.constant(2)
cons3 = cons1 + cons2
# instead of sess.run(cons3)
cons3.eval()
```

Variables

When training a model, we use variables to hold and update the parameters. Variables are like in-memory buffers containing tensors. All tensors we used previously were constant tensors, not variables.

Variables are managed or maintained by the session object. Variables persist between sessions, which is useful because tensor and operation objects are immutable:

```
# tensor variables
 W1 = tf.ones((3,3))
W2 = tf.Variable(tf.zeros((3,3)), name="weights")

 with tf.Session() as sess:
   print(sess.run(W1))
   sess.run(tf.global_variables_initializer())
   print(sess.run(W2))
```

The preceding code gives the following output:

```
[[ 1.  1.  1.] [ 1.  1.  1.] [ 1.  1.  1.]]
[[ 0.  0.  0.] [ 0.  0.  0.] [ 0.  0.  0.]]
```

TensorFlow variables must be initialized before they have values, which is in contrast with constant tensors:

```
# Variable objects can be initialized from constants or random values
W = tf.Variable(tf.zeros((2,2)), name="weights")
R = tf.Variable(tf.random_normal((2,2)), name="random_weights")

with tf.Session() as sess:
    # Initializes all variables with specified values.
```

```
sess.run(tf.initialize_all_variables())
print(sess.run(W))
print(sess.run(R))
```

The preceding code gives this output:

```
[[ 0.   0.] [ 0.   0.]]
[[ 0.65469146 -0.97390586] [-2.39198709  0.76642162]]

state = tf.Variable(0, name="counter")
new_value = tf.add(state, tf.constant(1))
update = tf.assign(state, new_value)

with tf.Session() as sess:
    sess.run(tf.initialize_all_variables())
    print(sess.run(state))
    for _ in range(3):
        sess.run(update)
        print(sess.run(state))
```

The preceding code gives the following output:

```
0  1  2  3
```

Fetching variable states:

```
input1 = tf.constant(5.0)
input2 = tf.constant(6.0)
input3 = tf.constant(7.0)
intermed = tf.add(input2, input3)
mul = tf.multiply(input1, intermed)

# Calling sess.run(var) on a tf.Session() object retrieves its value. Can
retrieve multiple variables simultaneously with sess.run([var1, var2])
with tf.Session() as sess:
    result = sess.run([mul, intermed])
    print(result)
```

The preceding code gives this output:

```
[65.0, 13.0]
```

Scope

TensorFlow models may have hundreds of variables. tf.variable_scope() provides a simple name.

To manage the complexity of models and break down into unique pieces, TensorFlow has scopes. Scopes are extremely simple and help when using TensorBoard. Scopes can also be nested inside of other scopes:

```
with tf.variable_scope("foo"):
    with tf.variable_scope("bar"):
        v = tf.get_variable("v", [1])
 assert v.name == "foo/bar/v:0"

 with tf.variable_scope("foo"):
    v = tf.get_variable("v", [1])
    tf.get_variable_scope().reuse_variables()
    v1 = tf.get_variable("v", [1])
 assert v1 == v
```

The following example shows how to use the reuse option to understand the behavior of `get_variable`:

```
#reuse is false
 with tf.variable_scope("foo"):
    n = tf.get_variable("n", [1])
 assert v.name == "foo/n:0"

 #Reuse is true
 with tf.variable_scope("foo"):
    n = tf.get_variable("n", [1])
 with tf.variable_scope("foo", reuse=True):
    v1 = tf.get_variable("n", [1])
 assert v1 == n
```

Data input

Input external data to TensorFlow objects:

```
a = np.zeros((3,3))
ta = tf.convert_to_tensor(a)
with tf.Session() as sess:
   print(sess.run(ta))
```

The preceding code gives the following output:

```
[[ 0. 0. 0.] [ 0. 0. 0.] [ 0. 0. 0.]]
```

Placeholders and feed dictionaries

Using `tf.convert_to_tensor()` to input data is convenient but it doesn't scale. Use `tf.placeholder` variables (dummy nodes that provide entry points for data to a computational graph). A `feed_dict` is a Python dictionary mapping:

```
input1 = tf.placeholder(tf.float32)
 input2 = tf.placeholder(tf.float32)
 output = tf.multiply(input1, input2)

with tf.Session() as sess:
    print(sess.run([output], feed_dict={input1:[5.], input2:[6.]}))
```

The preceding code gives this output:

```
[array([ 30.], dtype=float32)]
```

Auto differentiation

Auto differentiation is also known as **algorithmic differentiation**, which is an automatic way of numerically computing the derivatives of a function. It is helpful for computing gradients, Jacobians, and Hessians for use in applications such as numerical optimization. Backpropagation algorithm is an implementation of the reverse mode of automatic differentiation for calculating the gradient.

In the following example, using the `mnist` dataset, we calculate the loss using one of the `loss` functions. The question is: how do we fit the model to the data?

We can use `tf.train.Optimizer` and create an optimizer. `tf.train.Optimizer.minimize(loss, var_list)` adds an optimization operation to the computational graph and automatic differentiation computes gradients without user input:

```
import TensorFlow  as tf

# get mnist dataset
from TensorFlow .examples.tutorials.mnist import input_data
data = input_data.read_data_sets("MNIST_data/", one_hot=True)

# x represents image with 784 values as columns (28*28), y represents
output digit
x = tf.placeholder(tf.float32, [None, 784])
y = tf.placeholder(tf.float32, [None, 10])
```

```
# initialize weights and biases [w1,b1][w2,b2]
numNeuronsInDeepLayer = 30
w1 = tf.Variable(tf.truncated_normal([784, numNeuronsInDeepLayer]))
b1 = tf.Variable(tf.truncated_normal([1, numNeuronsInDeepLayer]))
w2 = tf.Variable(tf.truncated_normal([numNeuronsInDeepLayer, 10]))
b2 = tf.Variable(tf.truncated_normal([1, 10]))

# non-linear sigmoid function at each neuron
def sigmoid(x):
    sigma = tf.div(tf.constant(1.0), tf.add(tf.constant(1.0),
tf.exp(tf.negative(x))))
    return sigma

# starting from first layer with wx+b, then apply sigmoid to add non-
linearity
z1 = tf.add(tf.matmul(x, w1), b1)
a1 = sigmoid(z1)
z2 = tf.add(tf.matmul(a1, w2), b2)
a2 = sigmoid(z2)

# calculate the loss (delta)
loss = tf.subtract(a2, y)

# derivative of the sigmoid function der(sigmoid)=sigmoid*(1-sigmoid)
def sigmaprime(x):
    return tf.multiply(sigmoid(x), tf.subtract(tf.constant(1.0),
sigmoid(x)))

# automatic differentiation
cost = tf.multiply(loss, loss)
step = tf.train.GradientDescentOptimizer(0.1).minimize(cost)

acct_mat = tf.equal(tf.argmax(a2, 1), tf.argmax(y, 1))
acct_res = tf.reduce_sum(tf.cast(acct_mat, tf.float32))

sess = tf.InteractiveSession()
sess.run(tf.global_variables_initializer())

for i in range(10000):
    batch_xs, batch_ys = data.train.next_batch(10)
    sess.run(step, feed_dict={x: batch_xs,
                              y: batch_ys})
    if i % 1000 == 0:
        res = sess.run(acct_res, feed_dict=
        {x: data.test.images[:1000],
         y: data.test.labels[:1000]})
        print(res)
```

TensorBoard

TensorFlow has a powerful built-in visualization tool called **TensorBoard**. It allows developers to interpret, visualize, and debug computational graphs. To visualize graph and metrics automatically in TensorBoard, TensorFlow writes events related to the execution of a computational graph to a particular folder.

This example shows a computational graph of the analysis done earlier:

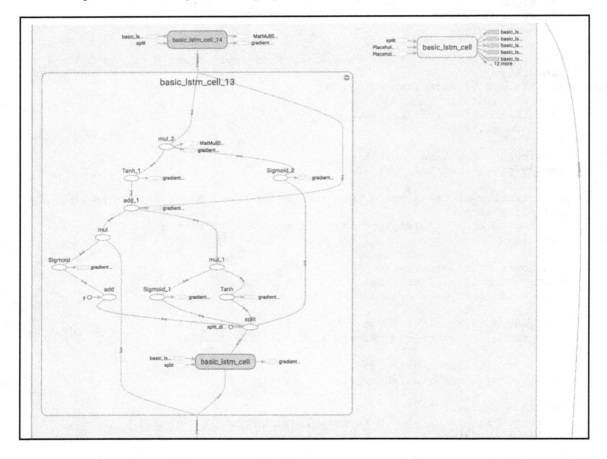

To examine the graph, click on the graph tab on the top panel of TensorBoard. If the graph has several nodes, visualizing it in a single view can be hard. To make our visualization more accessible, we can organize the related operations into groups using `tf.name_scope` with specific names.

Index